COPING WITH PRISON

Also available from Cassell:

Beta Copley and Barbara Forryan
Therapeutic Work with Children and Young People

Hans-Joachim Schulze and Wolfgang Wirth (eds)
Who Cares? Social Service Organizations and their Users

Roger Hadley and Roger Clough
Care in Chaos: Frustration and Challenge in Community Care

Coping with Prison

A Guide to Practitioners on the Realities of Imprisonment

STEVE GRAVETT

CASSELL

Cassell
Wellington House
125 Strand
London WC2R 0BB

Cassell & Continuum
370 Lexington Avenue
New York
NY 10017-6550

www.cassell.co.uk

First published 1999

British Library Cataloguing-in-Publication Data
A catalogue record for this book is available from the British Library.

ISBN   0-304-70475-X (hardback)   *20207743*
             0-304-70476-8 (paperback)

Designed and typeset by Kenneth Burnley, Wirral, Cheshire
Printed and bound in Great Britain by Redwood Books, Trowbridge, Wiltshire

Contents

Foreword

There are few subjects about which so many people hold strong views, often based on very superficial knowledge, as imprisonment. Those who are committed or sentenced to imprisonment for the first time will, inevitably, find difficulty in coming to terms with the deprivation of liberty that it entails, and their relatives and friends will find it equally difficult to understand exactly what life is like inside a prison, including the meaning of the various procedures and rules that govern imprisonment, many of which may affect them in some form or another.

As this book outlines, the first procedure should be a formal induction programme, designed to explain the routine and layout of the prison, the rules and regulations that prisoners must observe, the procedures governing various processes such as applying for visits, and, most important of all, a needs assessment to determine what work could and should be done to help the prisoner to remain a law-abiding citizen on release. There is a bewildering amount of information to absorb, and, on all too many occasions, I come across examples of prisoners who have been inadequately briefed, and who either miss out on opportunities, or break some rule or other, through ignorance.

This book, which has been researched with considerable care, serves a dual purpose, in that I am sure that it will prove to be just as valuable a reference for prisoners as for those who wish to understand the minutiae of imprisonment. It will serve as a primer for prison staff, who cannot be expected to remember all the details of every procedure, and who will welcome a source that is always at hand. Certainly a copy will be on my shelves, and I am only sorry that it was not available when I took up my post.

I am particularly pleased to note that the overall aim of the Prison Service is set out, because I believe that providing full, purposeful and active days for prisoners, aimed at preparing them for release, honours that far better than keeping prisoners locked in their cells all day. An informed prisoner, who can understand just what staff can do with and for him or her, is more likely to be a settled prisoner. Relatives and friends who know something of the conditions and treatment that prisoners undergo, are more likely to find it easier to cope with being victims of imprisonment themselves. These factors contribute to positive and constructive relationships between staff and prisoners, the bedrock of any well-ordered prison. I am sure that this book will make an important contribution to this process, and Steve Gravett is to be thanked and congratulated on his initiative, with which I wish every success.

Sir David Ramsbotham
HM Chief Inspector of Prisons

Preface

Sentencing someone to prison is the most serious punishment available to the courts. The powers of the Magistrates' Court are limited to a sentence of six months for a single offence, with an overall maximum of twelve months, if imposing a consecutive sentence.

If committed to the Crown Court there are no restrictions, and a life sentence can be imposed for the most serious offences. Imprisonment is only, according to the Criminal Justice Act 1991, for serious or violent offenders.

Since 1895 the official aim of the prison system has been to 'encourage and assist prisoners to lead a good and useful life'. In 1979 the May Committee proposed the notion of 'positive custody', but the modest concept of 'humane containment' was seen by others to be a more realistic approach. In 1988 the Home Office introduced its Statement of Purpose, which is prominently displayed in all establishments and reflects the official purpose of lawful custody.

Lord Justice Woolf concluded in 1991, after listening to the evidence of those involved in a series of prison disturbances, 'that their actions were a response to the manner in which they were treated by the prison system'. In essence they felt a lack of justice.

The only way to achieve justice in prisons, Lord Woolf concluded, was for the Prison Service to provide the following:

- a humane regime, which includes decent living conditions, physical exercise, purposeful activities, association and food;
- reasoned explanations for all decisions that affect individual prisoners;
- fair procedures for dealing with prisoners' grievances and perceived misbehaviour;
- security, control and justice;
- reasonable conditions and satisfactory relationships.

The Prison Service has also published its Vision, which is as follows:

Our vision is to provide a service, through both directly managed and contracted prisons, of which the public can be proud, and which will be regarded as a standard of excellence around the world.

The Prison Service has committed itself publicly to 'Fairness, Respect and Openness'. The main values it promises to honour are as follows:

- *Integrity*
  Integrity is fundamental to everything we do.
  We will meet our legal obligations, act with honesty and openness, and exercise effective stewardship of public money and assets.
- *Commitment*
  Commitment by our staff and to our staff.
  Staff are the most important asset of the Prison Service. They will be empowered to develop and use their skills and abilities to the full, while being held accountable for their performance.

Teamwork will be encouraged.

Staff will be treated with fairness, respect and openness.

Their safety and well-being will be a prime concern.

- *Care for prisoners*

Prisoners will be treated with fairness, justice and respect as individuals.

Their punishment is deprivation of liberty and they are entitled to certain recognised standards while in prison.

They will be given reasons for decisions, and, where possible, involved in discussions about matters affecting them.

In working with prisoners, we will involve their families and others in the community as fully as possible.

- *Equality of opportunity*

We are committed to equality of opportunity and the elimination of discrimination on improper grounds.

- *Innovation and improvement*

Innovation and improvement are essential to the success of the Service, requiring the acceptance of change and the delivery of continuing improvements in quality and efficiency.

In 1998 a report titled the *Prison Service Review* recommended to the Prisons Board that the existing 'Purpose, Vision, Goals and Values' should be clarified and replaced by a 'Prison Service Strategic Framework'. This revised framework would comprise an aim, objectives and a set of principles which were crisper and more succinct. The objectives would be clear standards capable of being quantified and costed. The proposed Revised Prison Service Strategic Framework is as follows:

Aim

Effective execution of the sentences of the courts so as to reduce re-offending and protect the public.

Objectives

- Protect the public by holding those committed by the courts in a safe, decent and healthy environment.
- Reduce crime by providing constructive regimes which address offending behaviour, improve educational and work skills and promote law-abiding behaviour in custody and after release.

Principles

In undertaking its work the Prison Service will:

- Deal fairly, correctly and openly with staff, prisoners and all who come into contact with us.
- Work effectively with other bodies.
- Help prisoners to take responsibility for their behaviour, to respect the rights of others to maintain links with their families and the wider community.

- Value the contribution of staff, ensuring that they are effectively prepared and supported in the work they do.
- Obtain best value from resources provided.

ACKNOWLEDGEMENTS

My thanks to Richard Tilt, the Director General of the Prison Service, who kindly gave permission for me to write this book and reproduce several forms.

Any views expressed in this book are solely those of the author and should not be interpreted as official Prison Service policy.

HOW TO USE THIS BOOK

This book contains a wealth of information and should prove to be a valuable source of reference for everyone involved in offering advice and guidance to inmates and their families.

A comprehensive *index* has been included to enable key words and sections of explanatory information to be found easily, and the *appendix of documents* gives examples of forms referred to in the text.

Readers who wish to familiarise themselves with the penal system will find the *case studies* helpful in bringing alive the material in each chapter. They follow the lives of four fictitious but representative inmates as their sentences progress, and provide an element of continuity throughout the book.

Educationalists and students of penal affairs will find the *checklists* at the end of each chapter a useful revision aid. The *discussion points* are intended to stimulate thought and provide a method of relating the material to current penal policy.

This book is intended to be a comprehensive handbook for professional colleagues, students and inmates alike. The pace of change in the penal field is considerable and some updating will no doubt prove inevitable as new legislation and case law regularly impact on penal practice.

The male gender has been used thoughout for ease of expression and consistency. Unless mentioned specifically, the entitlements and practice are identical in the case of female inmates.

This book is dedicated to all the victims of crime: those unfortunate individuals who directly suffer the trauma and distress of criminal behaviour, their extended families and friends who are adversely affected, and finally the taxpayer, who has to finance our expensive Criminal Justice System. As a society we must succeed in looking after inmates humanely, treat them fairly, and help them to lead law-abiding lives in custody and after release; otherwise there will never be fewer victims.

Any suggestions for improving this handbook will always be warmly welcomed by the author, who can be contacted courtesy of the publisher.

STEVE GRAVETT
Spring 1999

CHAPTER 1

The Culture

FACING UP TO REALITY

Once the cell door clangs shut each occupant is left alone in a $10' \times 6'$ cell which is now home for the next few days, weeks, months or even years. It is claustrophobic and basic: a metal bed, a mattress, a small table, a notice-board for pin-ups, and a locker for clothing and personal belongings. There are no curtains, the walls are cream, the floor is covered in lino and there is a small mat. In the corner of the cell behind a courtesy screen lies a toilet and wash hand basin. A single barred window looks out on to another grey prison wing containing rows of identical cells.

Inmates feel acutely their sense of loss: the loss of freedom and separation from loved ones. They are conscious of a complete lack of control over their lives, of becoming totally dependent on others, and feel they have become simply another statistic. This is the pain of imprisonment: deprivation of liberty. This is the punishment the courts decided they deserve.

In prison the staff appear to have enormous control over the lives of inmates, who in turn feel helpless and vulnerable. The system decides when they can get up, where and what they eat, how they spend their time, and whether or when their family and friends are allowed to visit.

Sharing a cell is a mixed blessing. It solves the problem of loneliness, but at the expense of any privacy. Spending time in a confined space with a stranger demands tolerance and flexibility. No wonder most inmates are keen to have a single cell at the earliest opportunity, a highly prized privilege, but one that has to be earned.

The key to survival is knowledge. The sooner newcomers understand how the system works, the quicker they can adjust to custodial life. Only then can they take away something positive from the experience.

ADJUSTING TO CUSTODY

A person who enters prison or Young Offenders' Institution for the first time will feel apprehensive and disorientated. Initially he is taken to Reception, where the process is designed to assess his needs, make a record of essential information, store any property not permitted in possession, and in the case of a male sentenced prisoner, issue with prison clothing.

On reception the following procedures are carried out:

- The warrant which accompanies the inmate from court is checked to make certain that the establishment has authority to hold the individual in custody.
- All clothing and property are thoroughly searched.
- The inmate is strip searched in a private area, out of sight of other prisoners and officers of the opposite sex, for any contraband or offensive weapons.
- A member of the health care team sees all new receptions to identify any immediate medical needs, to advise about the range of medical facilities available, and to assess the risk of self-harm or suicide occurring, seeking medical assistance as necessary.
- Within 24 hours the Medical Officer carries out a full medical examination.
- A full record of all property and money brought into the establishment is made, and the inmate asked to verify and certify that the details have been accurately recorded on his property card.
- All new receptions are allowed to keep certain items in their possession on the understanding they are held entirely at the inmate's own risk. It is important they consider the risks inherent in keeping a valuable item that may prove irresistible to dishonest inmates. A full list of the items permitted in each establishment is available in the form of a published statement.
- A Prisoners Information Pack, containing relevant information about the establishment's routines and local rules, is provided.
- A hot bath or shower, and a meal (or snack and drink) will be provided while inmates are being processed through reception.
- On reception from court, inmates are allowed the opportunity to make two brief telephone calls at public expense to relatives or their legal adviser, to inform them of their whereabouts.
- Routine personal information is requested and entered into the F2050 case record, which includes details about religion, ethnic origin and next of kin.
- Inmates who do not qualify to wear their own clothing are issued with sufficient clothing to meet their needs. This includes a comb, toothbrush, toothpaste, soap, towel, nailbrush and a pair of shoes. Shaving equipment is issued to men and sanitary protection items to women.
- All convicted prisoners are photographed; the photograph is routinely updated every two years and whenever a change in appearance occurs. Remand prisoners and those held under the Immigration Act 1971 are not normally photographed unless there are good security reasons, or questions about identity.
- The fingerprints of sentenced prisoners are routinely taken, but only exceptionally for civil prisoners (i.e. a person committed to prison for a non-criminal offence).
- A reception letter is issued so that each new inmate can write to family or friends, at public expense.

ATTENDING THE RECEPTION BOARD

Once the reception process has been completed, a new inmate is allocated a prison number which remains with him throughout his sentence. This number must appear on all outgoing letters. Similarly, family and friends need to include the prison number on all letters they send in, otherwise they run the risk of mail going astray internally, or being held up.

The day following reception into custody is when the Reception Board is held, excepting Sundays. Practice varies between establishments; in a local prison a formal Reception Board is normally held, but in other establishments it is common practice to hold a series of interviews with new receptions. The purpose of the Reception Board is to check factual details relating to the inmate's custody, advise of a release date, confirm that the security classification is appropriate, and for remand prisoners find out whether they want to undertake any paid work. Any questions or problems are dealt with, and an appointment arranged with the seconded probation officer, legal aid officer, personal officer and the governor's representative.

LODGING AN APPEAL

Anyone who disagrees with the decision of the court is entitled to appeal to a higher court against that decision. Unless the appeal is against a decision made by the Magistrates' Court the permission of the court has to be obtained before an appeal can be made.

There are time limits which determine when an appeal can be lodged. These apply from the date of conviction:

- an appeal to the Crown Court must be lodged at the Magistrates' Court within 21 days;
- a notice of leave to appeal against a Crown Court decision must be lodged at the Crown Court within 28 days;
- an appeal from the Court of Appeal Criminal Division (CACD) to the House of Lords has to be made within 14 days, but to succeed it must be based on a point of law.

The Legal Aid Officer sees all potential appellants on reception, and if they are not legally represented he can arrange for them to have a solicitor. He is able to help inmates make an application for Legal Aid and advise about the time limits for lodging an appeal. He keeps a range of advice leaflets in different languages as well as a stock of all the official forms necessary for making an application for Legal Aid or lodging an appeal. If an inmate is not represented by a solicitor he may still be able to receive legal advice under the Green Form Scheme. Once Legal Aid has been approved prisoners can receive professional advice and assistance in connection with an appeal.

MAKING PRACTICAL ARRANGEMENTS

Going into custody means tying up lots of loose ends. An inmate may not know how long he will be inside if being held on remand and there will be an anxious wait for the outcome of court proceedings. If employed, he should not delay in informing his employer, who may agree to a period of extended leave of absence until the outcome is known. Once sentence is passed, an employer may be willing to keep the prisoner's job open, particularly if the sentence is short, provided the offence is not one that excludes the inmate from resuming his job.

An inmate running his own business will be anxious to make arrangements for someone, perhaps his spouse or business partner, to keep his affairs in order. He should be encouraged to seek professional advice from a solicitor and an accountant because he will not be permitted to continue to run a business as a convicted prisoner. An unconvicted prisoner is allowed extra letters and telephone calls in order to keep business interests alive, but once convicted this can only continue for a limited time to enable him to wind up the business or make other suitable arrangements.

For a single parent the priority is making suitable arrangements with family or friends for the care of any children. Child benefit can be transferred to a responsible adult during custody, provided the Benefits Agency is informed. The local Social Services Department can offer advice; they have a duty to provide suitable care for the children if satisfactory arrangements cannot be made.

If an inmate gives up his accommodation on entering prison, or is evicted while in prison, he faces the problem of finding somewhere suitable to store furniture and possessions. Unless family or friends are willing to remove and store them, there may be no alternative but to ask a removal firm to provide storage facilities: an expensive solution.

Inmates need to consider how they plan to meet any other commitments such as repayments to a hire purchase company or bank. If they are unable to keep up the payments because of their imprisonment, they should write to the lenders asking them to reschedule the loans.

KEEPING THE PRISONER'S HOME

Keeping a home while in custody is a high priority, particularly if an inmate lives alone and there is no one to assume responsibility for claiming the appropriate benefits.

A tenant living in a rented house owned by the council, a private landlord or a housing association, and intending to return there on release, may be eligible to claim housing benefit. The conditions for qualifying are:

Sentenced prisoners serving
(a) under 13 weeks in custody are eligible to claim housing benefit;
(b) over 13 weeks in custody are not eligible for housing benefit for any of the period spent in prison.

Remand prisoners
(a) are eligible to claim housing benefit for up to 52 weeks;
(b) convicted but not sentenced are eligible for benefit for up to 52 weeks.

A claim needs to be made as soon as a person is received into custody, since claims take time to process and all claimants are obliged to report any changes in their circumstances to the Benefits Agency. If the rent on the property is above the average in the area, the housing benefit allowed may be insufficient to cover the full cost of the rent.

If this is the case a prisoner can take the following steps:

* write to his landlord;
* approach the council for a housing benefit claim form;
* obtain from the council a form to claim exemption from Council Tax; the criteria for eligibility are similar to those of housing benefit.

If the inmate's family or partner are still living in his home, they should be encouraged to seek advice and help about making a claim from the Benefits Agency, the Housing Department, a Housing Advice Centre and the Citizens Advice Bureau.

The range of help available to inmates who have a mortgage is more limited. In the case of sentenced prisoners and those awaiting sentence there is no help available whatsoever. Remand prisoners awaiting trial can apply to the Benefits Agency Office for help. No one is eligible for assistance during the first eight weeks and only half of the interest payments will be met for the next 18 weeks. Once an inmate has been in custody for 26 weeks the interest payments will be met in full.

Anyone with a mortgage can easily run up a sizable debt. It is sensible to write to the mortgage society or bank to explain the circumstances and ask to reschedule payments so an inmate is only obliged to repay interest while in custody. He should seek expert guidance, including legal advice, if he is unable to meet mortgage payments, or arrange for them to be rescheduled or deferred until his discharge. Options available include letting or selling the property, but before reaching a final decision he should contact a solicitor, a housing aid centre or the Citizens Advice Bureau.

It is necessary to arrange with the water company to discontinue the service or waive charges for the time a prisoner is away. Similarly the gas and electricity companies should be asked to disconnect the supply to avoid liability for standing charges.

Finally, if a property is going to be empty for any length of time the landlord should be informed and arrangements made for a friend or relative to keep an eye on the building. It is advisable to drain the water, especially in winter, because domestic insurance policies normally exclude cover for 'loss of water' in homes unoccupied for more than one month.

FINDING A PRISONER

The family and friends of an inmate can discover which prison he has been taken to by contacting the court where he appeared. Remand prisoners are normally held in the local prison or remand centre which is closest to the court that remanded them in custody. Once sentenced they are normally accommodated in a local prison until they have been fully assessed. Unless they are serving a short sentence it is normal to be moved elsewhere and this can be some distance from home.

If some time has elapsed, the Prisoner Location Service run by the Prison Service can help family and friends, but they will only deal with written requests for information. Anyone seeking information about an inmate's whereabouts will need to give as much information as possible, including reasons for wishing to make contact. The inmate will be approached for permission before any information is released to any enquirers.

The address to contact is: Prisoner Location Service, PO Box 2152, Birmingham B15 1SD.

HELP WITH TRAVEL COSTS

If an inmate's family is on a low income or in receipt of benefits, they will probably qualify for help with the cost of travelling to the establishment.

The Assisted Prison Visits Unit (APVU) will meet the costs of two visits every four weeks together with the cost of meals, and if unavoidable the cost of overnight accommodation for close relatives or a partner. A 'partner' means someone of the opposite sex who has been living with the inmate for at least four months, or who has a child from the relationship.

To qualify for help from the APVU the family need to meet the follow criteria:

- they are in receipt of Family Credit, Income Support or Disability Allowance;
- they have a low income, only slightly above Income Support levels.

They need to obtain explanatory leaflet Form 2022A and complete Form 2022 which is obtainable from a Benefits Agency office. It should be sent to the following address: Assisted Prison Visits Unit (APVU), PO Box 2152, Birmingham B15 1SD (telephone: 0121–626 2797).

The family should return the completed form to the APVU ten days before they plan to visit, in order to give the APVU time to send out their travelling expenses. In the case of sentenced prisoners they will need to send a copy of the visiting order when returning the form. Depending on how the family intend to travel, the APVU will send either a rail warrant, the money for the bus fare, or a mileage allowance of 10p per mile.

If the family have already made a visit and met the costs themselves, they can claim a refund if they can produce proof of the travelling costs they incurred, and make their claim within four weeks of making the visit.

Other allowances that can be claimed include:

- a meals allowance, provided the time they are away from home exceeds five hours;
- the cost of overnight accommodation, provided the round trip takes more than 15 hours;
- the cost of overnight accommodation if a visitor is too ill to travel the distances involved in one day and their doctor provides a note verifying this;

- unavoidable childminding costs;
- an escorting allowance can be claimed if a relative is too young or too ill to travel alone.

The APVU also meet travelling costs if approval is given for a special visit, or the inmate goes on accumulated visits.

A *special visit* is granted in addition to the normal visiting entitlement if an urgent and exceptional domestic problem arises.

Accumulated visits are approved when the distances involved make it impractical for a family to visit and the inmate is temporarily transferred to an establishment nearer home for the express purpose of receiving visits. The pressure on the prison estate is currently so intense that it is becoming increasingly difficult for this to happen. An alternative is for relatives to save up the visiting orders to make the journey worthwhile, and take several visits on successive days.

KNOWING THE SECURITY CATEGORY

Following sentence and committal to prison, a careful assessment is made during the first week to determine how likely an inmate is to escape, and if successful the degree of risk he poses to the general public if unlawfully at large. This review considers matters relevant to the offence, the length of sentence imposed by the court, previous convictions and any history of escaping from lawful custody, before reaching a decision about an inmate's security category.

Apart from Category A prisoners, who are classified and managed centrally by Prison Service Headquarters, all these assessments are carried out by staff in the Observation, Classification and Allocation unit (OCA). They decide on the appropriate security category before allocating inmates to a suitable establishment (see Figure 1.1).

All adult male sentenced prisoners are placed into one of four security categories as recommended in the *Mountbatten Report* in 1967.

Category A
'Prisoners for whom escape would be highly dangerous to the public or police, or to the security of the nation.' The prison must try to make escape impossible for anyone held as a Category A prisoner.

Category B
'Prisoners for whom the very highest conditions of security are not necessary, but for whom escape must be made very difficult.' These inmates must be held in very secure conditions with high priority given at all times to holding them securely in custody.

Category C
'Prisoners who cannot be trusted in open conditions but who do not have the will or resources to make a determined escape attempt.' They are not thought likely to make a determined effort to escape but are not yet ready to be trusted in open conditions.

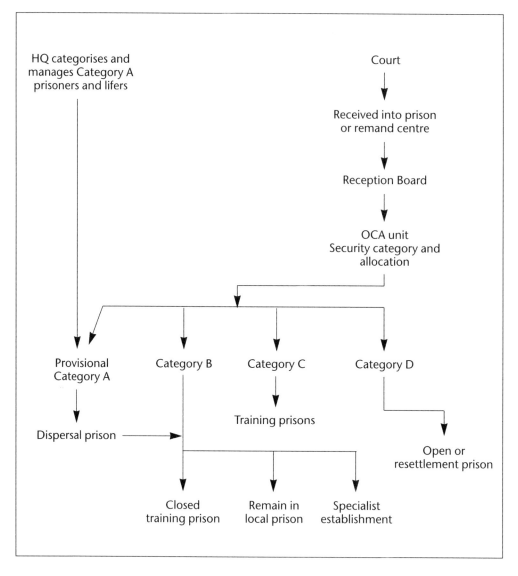

Figure 1.1: The classification and allocation process

Category D
'Prisoners who can be trusted to serve their sentence in open conditions.' They are considered trustworthy and unlikely to abscond, and have proved able to exercise self-control, or have completed a period of temporary release elsewhere.

Women and young offenders are not security categorised unless they meet the criteria for Category A.

Only about 1 per cent of prisoners are classified Category A, 19 per cent are Category B, 48 per cent Category C and 17 per cent are Category D. Normally about 15 per cent are awaiting categorisation at any given time and any unsentenced prisoner is assumed to be a Category B unless he has been identified as a provisional Category A due to the seriousness of his alleged offence.

Under Prison Rule 3 'unconvicted prisoners shall be kept out of contact with convicted prisoners as far this can reasonably be done'.

Security categories are important as they affect where inmates are held, the quality of regime available to them, and may affect their chances of getting parole.

Every security categorisation should be reviewed annually throughout an inmate's sentence. As the release date draws nearer, the likelihood of being recategorised increases if the inmate has acted responsibly and not been a source of concern to the establishment's Security Department.

Although inmates are not given detailed reasons for their security categorisation, it is normally fairly clear how the decision has been reached. If an inmate feels aggrieved he can use the Request and Complaint system to make a complaint. If the correct procedure has not been followed or the decision is legally *unreasonable,* it can be challenged by way of judicial review.

Criteria for categorisation

Inmates are normally considered suitable for Category D, unless their circumstances fall within the following criteria:

- serving over 12 months for an offence of violence;
- convicted of a sexual offence;
- previous convictions for violence or sexual offences, unless part of the sentence has been served in open conditions;
- previous convictions for arson or importing drugs;
- recent history of absconding or escaping.

If an inmate has served a previous sentence in Category D conditions it is unlikely he would be subsequently placed in higher conditions of security unless the current offence is clearly much more serious. Civil prisoners and fine defaulters are usually categorised D.

Inmates are normally considered suitable for Category C unless the following conditions apply:

- serving over seven years for a violent or sexual offence;
- previous sentences served of over seven years for violent or sexual offences, unless part of the sentence has been served in Category C conditions;
- current sentence is for more than ten years;
- recent history of absconding or escaping.

Inmates are normally placed in Category B if they have been convicted of a serious violent, sexual or drug-related offence.

Anyone on remand awaiting trial, or convicted but awaiting sentence, is placed in Category U, meaning unclassified, and is usually treated as requiring Category B accommodation. The only exceptions are those provisionally categorised A who are dealt with by Prison Service Headquarters.

BEING A CIVIL PRISONER

An inmate is described as a civil prisoner if he is sent to prison for any reason other than for committing a criminal offence.

The range of offences include:

- disobeying a *maintenance order* made by a judge to provide financial support to a spouse;
- failing to obey an *affiliation order* to make payments to support children;
- not paying debt, known as a *civil debt,* when a court has made an order;
- failing to pay costs, or money due under a *legal aid contribution order*;
- being in *contempt of court.*

Under Prison Rules civil prisoners are treated as convicted prisoners. However, Prison Rule 63 makes it clear they must be given the same privileges as unconvicted prisoners in respect of:

- visits, letters and telephone calls, which includes contact with their legal adviser under Rule 37A;
- associating with other classes of prisoner;
- the right to wear their own clothes.

Provided they wear prison clothing, civil prisoners wishing to mix with other prisoners may be allowed to do so.

The length of time spent in custody will depend on whether they qualify for early release. The court may have fixed the release date when they made the committal to prison; in these circumstances the whole of the sentence will be served. If they qualify for early release, the release date will be halfway through the sentence if the sentence is for 12 months or less, otherwise it will be after two-thirds of the sentence has been completed.

Anyone committed to prison for contempt of court has a right of appeal provided they serve notice of appeal within 14 days of the date of committal. The Legal Aid Officer or a solicitor will give guidance about obtaining legal advice. A prisoner acting for himself can write directly to: The Registrar of Civic Appeals, Royal Courts of Justice, Strand, London WC2A 2LL.

UNDERSTANDING THE PRISON SYSTEM

Each establishment is given a security classification which reflects its ability to prevent prisoners from escaping. If an inmate is considered to be a high security risk he will be classified Category A and held in a dispersal prison or a special secure unit (SSU). High-risk prisoners have extra restrictions placed on their visitors who are vetted by the police and prison authorities before they are permitted to visit. Category A prisoners are closely scrutinised by staff and subject to surveillance by security cameras. They are always escorted outside the wing by prison officers, dog handlers constantly patrol and they can expect to be frequently searched. Their cells are subject to random searches and they are required to change cells regularly. At night the cell light is kept on, albeit dimmed, and clothing has to be placed outside the cell.

The Category A estate

Following the *Learmont Report* into the escape of three Category A prisoners from HMP Parkhurst, security arrangements were reviewed and perimeter security upgraded in all those prisons holding high-risk prisoners. The size of the Category A estate was reduced in 1997 to 13 establishments, and apart from Hull, which has a specially secure unit, it includes Belmarsh, Frankland, Full Sutton, Long Lartin, Wakefield, Whitemoor, Altcourse, Bristol, Doncaster, High Down, Manchester and Woodhill.

Locals and closed training prisons

All local prisons and remand centres are Category B. In addition certain closed training prisons holding prisoners serving lengthy sentences are referred to as Category B trainers. Sentenced prisoners are held at a local prison until they have been classified and a decision made about where to allocate them. This process takes into account where their home is, any particular medical and regime recommendations, and which establishments have spaces. This practical constraint tends to severely restrict the range of options available to prison staff working in OCA units and means some prisoners are allocated to prisons a long way from their families.

The population pressures show no sign of easing in the foreseeable future. The prison population increased by 35 per cent during the period 1994–97 and the latest White Paper 'Protecting the Public' suggests this trend is set to continue.

Some closed training prisons have a clearly defined role: in HMP Albany accredited sex offender treatment programmes are available for anyone who has been placed on Rule 43 elsewhere. Others like HMP Grendon have developed a unique therapeutic regime for those wishing to address their offending behaviour. If an inmate has a special need and wants to be considered for such a placement he can approach prison staff or the medical officer.

Semi-closed and open prisons

The Category C estate consists mainly of training prisons which vary from those with a secure perimeter wall and closed cellular accommodation to semi-open dormitory-styled establishments with a perimeter fence.

Open prisons do not rely on any physical security measures apart from a perimeter fence. The responsibility lies firmly with the individual to keep to the rules and not abscond or abuse trust, using the opportunity to prepare for his return to society. This can be quite daunting for those coming to the end of a long sentence or in the final stages of a life sentence. Inmates serving short sentences or in prison for the first time are likely to spend part of their sentence in open conditions.

Caring for young offenders

Young offenders are normally sent to a Young Offender Institution unless they are under 17 years old and have committed a very serious crime. If the court decides the appropriate sentence is a life sentence or detention under Section 53 of the Children and Young Persons Act 1933 (that is to be detained during Her Majesty's Pleasure), Prison Service Headquarters may decide that a transfer to a secure facility managed by the Social Services Department or to a Youth Treatment Centre run by the Department of Health is more appropriate.

Catering for the needs of women

Women and girls are catered for in 15 female establishments in the country. The likelihood is that they will be a long way from their family and friends.

Female establishments are located in the following areas:

Local prisons
Risley (Cheshire), Pucklechurch (Bristol), Low Newton (Durham), Holloway (London), New Hall (Wakefield).

Closed prisons
Styal (Cheshire), Cookham Wood (Kent), Bullwood Hall (Essex), F and H Wings in Durham, Send (Surrey).

Open prisons
Askham Grange (York), Drake Hall (Staffordshire), East Sutton Park (Kent).

Females who present a high security risk are moved to Durham or Bullwood Hall. Those needing psychiatric help are sent to Holloway, which has specialist facilities.

Within Holloway, Styal, New Hall and Askham Grange there are separate mother-and-baby units that cater for the special needs of women in the final stages of pregnancy. They can keep their babies with them for up to 18 months if it is judged to be in the child's best interests.

CASE STUDIES

Each chapter concludes with four fictional case studies which are used to show a cross-section of problems that face inmates and to highlight issues raised in the preceding text.

Rudd Basho, Young Offender

Rudd Basho is a single West Indian youngster aged 17 who lives at home with his parents in west London. His pregnant girlfriend Lola is homeless and under the supervision of the Social Services Department. Rudd has been subject to a two-year probation order for theft and burglary but is commencing his first custodial sentence having been sentenced to 12 months Youth Custody for taking and driving away a vehicle. Rudd left school without gaining any qualifications and has not worked. He is genuinely fond of Lola and wants to provide for her and their child on release.

Peter Miles, Adult Offender

Peter Miles, in his early thirties, cohabits with his common-law wife and their three children. A regular offender, he has previously served three custodial sentences; he has convictions for threatening behaviour, assault, burglary and robbery, mostly drink-related. He is now involved in the drugs scene and his sentence of five years imprisonment is for the illegal importation of Class A drugs and for supplying them to young people. His relationship with his common-law wife is currently very strained as she struggles to support herself and their three small children.

Paddy Naughtie, Lifer

Paddy Naughtie is divorced and in his mid-fifties. He is a professional criminal who has completed 15 years of a life sentence for the murder of a night watchman while committing an armed robbery. His marriage broke up early in his sentence; his wife remarried but no longer keeps in contact. Apart from his mother, in her eighties and terminally ill with lung cancer, he is all alone. His father died two years ago and, following his death, Paddy suffered from depression and attempted suicide. He has developed a close relationship with a female penfriend who visits regularly and they intend to spend their future together after he is released.

Nicola Harrington, Female prisoner

Nicola Harrington is a single woman of 21 who comes from the London area. She has recently broken off a stormy relationship with her boyfriend because he was violent towards her and spent all their benefit on drugs and alcohol. Six months pregnant and without a home or job, she is living in a women's refuge with five others. Her mother was killed in a road accident when she was ten and she was in local authority care until she was 18. Apart from an older brother, with whom she lost contact when he emigrated to Australia two years ago, she has no living relatives. Nicola has numerous previous convictions for theft and one previous custodial sentence. She is independent and headstrong but was hoping to settle down with her boyfriend before things became intolerable. Since then she has returned to crime to support herself, but was recently arrested for shoplifting and is now serving 18 months' imprisonment.

CHECKLIST

- When are inmates allowed to wear their own clothing?
- How can inmates safeguard their home while in prison?
- What happens to valuable items of property brought into prison?
- How can a single parent care for his or her children in custody?
- Where can women with psychiatric problems receive assistance in custody?

- What are accumulated visits?
- How does an inmate qualify for a special visit?
- What are the responsibilities of the OCA unit?
- Which inmates are photographed on reception?
- What is the purpose of the Reception Board?
- What is a mother-and-baby unit?

- How does the Prisoner Location Service work?
- What is the Assisted Prison Visits Unit?
- Which prisoners qualify for open conditions?
- How often should an inmate's security category be reviewed?
- In which security category are the majority of adult prisoners placed?

DISCUSSION POINTS

1. The pain of imprisonment is deprivation of liberty. Should a sentenced prisoner be forced to wind up his business, thus depriving him of the means to support his family?

2. Examine the advantages and disadvantages of providing financial assistance for prisoners with their housing costs.

3. The process of determining security categories is clothed in secrecy. Consider whether current practice can be improved.

4. Examine the case for holding all Category A prisoners in a single establishment.

5. Consider the advantages and disadvantages of increasing the number of security categories, on the grounds that the Category C estate covers both closed and semi-open prisons. Should young offenders and women be given security categories?

6. 'Every woman who gives birth in prison should be allowed to keep the baby with her.' Discuss.

CHAPTER 2

Entitlements

KNOWING PRISONERS' ENTITLEMENTS

Every prison and young offender establishment is required to operate a system of privileges under Prison Rule 4 and Young Offender Institution Rule 7. They are also contained in Standing Order 4, called *Facilities*, which inmates are allowed to purchase.

European Prison Rule 45 states that

> prisoners shall be allowed to keep themselves informed regularly of the news by the reading of newspapers, periodicals, and other publications, by radio or television transmissions, by lectures or by any similar means as authorised by the administration. Special arrangements should be made to meet the needs of foreign nationals with linguistic difficulties.

The rules are clear regarding which items of personal property are allowed to be kept in possession. Practice varies widely, but the principle is that each inmate should have sufficient personal items in their cell to enable them to lead as normal a life in custody as is possible, bearing in mind the obvious constraints that life inside imposes.

Since the Standing Order was revised in 1992, the escapes of Category A prisoners from HMP Parkhurst and HMP Whitemoor led to two enquiries. The published report *Review of Prison Security in England and Wales and The Escape from Parkhurst Prison on Tuesday 3rd January 1995* by General Sir John Learmont KCB, CBE, otherwise known as the Learmont Report, led to the introduction of *volumetric control* of each prisoner's possessions. This specifies that the amount of property allowed in a cell must not be more than the equivalent of two transit boxes. With the introduction of the Incentive and Earned Privilege Scheme, certain items of property permitted in possession have to be earned as a privilege.

An inmate is allowed to have the following items in his cell:

- at least six newspapers and magazines. These must be ordered and sent in directly from a newsagent or publisher, unless he is in a Category C or D establishment;
- at least three books. These must be obtained directly from the publisher or bookshop, except in a Category C or D establishment;
- a combined sound system or radio, and either a record player, cassette player or

compact disc player. The cassette players may retain the recording facility as inmates are allowed to send out taped messages to their family and friends;

- a quantity of records, compact discs or cassettes, up to a maximum number decided by the local Governor. Unless an inmate is in a Category C or D establishment, commercially pre-recorded tapes must be sent in directly from an approved supplier.

A number of restrictions apply to the use of radios in establishments, mainly for security reasons as the prison authorities understandably do not want inmates overhearing prison and emergency service transmissions. A radio therefore has to conform to the following specifications:

(a) it has to be battery-operated, but it may have an internal mains adaptor which can be used in certain establishments which have in-cell electricity;

(b) it must be capable of receiving transmissions within the 88–108 MHz band, short wave transmissions between 1–18 MHz, and medium and long wave transmissions;

(c) an aerial attached to the radio is allowed;

(d) an earpiece socket is desirable as the Governor may require the use of an earpiece or headphones to prevent annoyance to other inmates. The Governor may also require the use of an earpiece with other sound equipment;

- smoking requisites: the limit for unconvicted prisoners is 137.5 grams of tobacco or 180 cigarettes. Convicted prisoners are limited to 62.5 grams of tobacco or 80 cigarettes. Tobacco is now supplied in standard packets of 25 grams, 12.5 grams or 5 grams. Inmates may have cigars instead of cigarettes if preferred;
- hobbies materials;
- games including electronic games, provided they do not have a data storage facility;
- writing and drawing materials;
- a wrist watch including one with an alarm function;
- a manual typewriter;
- a battery shaver;
- batteries for items allowed in possession;
- personal toiletries;
- a wedding ring or plain ring;
- one medallion or locket;
- religious items which have been authorised by the Governor;
- photographs, pictures and unglazed picture frames;
- greetings cards, provided they are not the padded variety;
- a calendar;
- a diary or personal organiser;
- an address book;
- phonecards;
- postage stamps.

These items can normally be sent in or handed in by friends and relatives, or purchased from earnings or private cash. Many Governors have used their discretion and introduced local restrictions for security reasons or as part of the Incentive and Earned Privilege Scheme.

SPENDING MONEY

Until recently there were restrictions on the amount of private cash inmates could spend as convicted prisoners in a twelve-month period. Since the Incentive and Earned Privilege Scheme was introduced the level of expenditure permitted is determined by which regime a prisoner is on.

Inmates on the *basic regime* are restricted to spending £2.50 each week from their private cash, equivalent to an annual level of £130 per annum. On the *standard regime* they can spend £10 each week from private cash, equivalent to £520 per annum. This is much higher than the previous annual limit even when the former hobbies allowance is included. Those on the *enhanced regime* can spend £30 each week from private cash, the equivalent of £1560 per annum. All inmates on the enhanced regime can be considered for any Enhanced Earnings Scheme which operates in the establishment.

The private cash limits for unconvicted prisoners are more generous. Any remand prisoners on the basic regime can spend £15 each week, and those on the standard regime £30 a week.

Every prison and Young Offender Institution (YOI) runs a shop, usually referred to as a canteen, where a wide range of items are stocked, including batteries, stamps, sweets, toiletries, tobacco, stationery and pens or biros. All inmate needs should be catered for including the preferences of ethnic minorities, who often have particular requirements when it comes to skin or hair care products. Ideally inmates should be able to visit the shop twice a week, but in practice few establishments are able to provide this level of service.

The following items can be purchased in the prison shop only:

- food and sweets
- phonecards
- tobacco (except unconvicted prisoners)
- batteries for use in items allowed in possession. In YOIs batteries can be sent in or handed in by relatives or friends.

EARNING POWER

All sentenced prisoners are required to work or attend classes. The minimum amount they will be paid is £4 per week. However, if there is no work available then the minimum rate of £2.50 weekly applies.

The average wage for those in employment is £7 per week. Each establishment has a pay scheme geared to its own needs, and rates vary accordingly. For instance, where there are industrial workshops producing products for Regime Services, the earnings scheme is likely to be linked to productivity with the most industrious earning £10 per week.

Instructors, party officers and teachers have discretion to make deductions from the normal party rate if inmates arrive late for work or classes, are lazy, or fail to meet the required standards of behaviour or performance. Major shortcomings can result in inmates being removed from the their place of work and facing a disciplinary charge.

Some prisons have introduced *enhanced earnings schemes* in certain workshops and on their farms, where improved productivity brings in extra revenue to the establishment. When private contract work is being undertaken it is usual to find an enhanced earnings schemes operating. The reason is that any income generated from private work can be credited to the establishment's budget, unlike revenue from products produced for the internal market. Governors facing budgetary pressure are keen to take advantage of the opportunity to work with the private sector and as a direct consequence increasing number of enhanced earnings schemes are being introduced.

Enhanced earnings schemes bring potential earnings of around £20 a week, depending on the individual's productivity. This compares favourably with the average wage received by employment inmates of £7.50 per week. One of the conditions of the Enhanced Earnings Scheme is that a small proportion of earnings, normally not less than £4 per week, has to be saved towards the inmate's discharge.

KEEPING IN TOUCH

Keeping in touch with family, friends and other people is very important. With the exception of inmates in conditions of maximum security, there has been a general relaxation of the rules in this area in recent years.

An unconvicted prisoner is allowed to send out as many letters as he wishes at his own expense, with two second-class letters being provided each week at public expense to help maintain outside contacts. A first-class letter is provided to all new receptions, irrespective of their legal status. Apart from provisional Category A prisoners, outgoing letters are not routinely read, but all incoming letters are opened to check they do not contain contraband.

Correspondence between an inmate and his legal adviser is privileged and is treated as confidential provided it is clearly marked *Prison Rule 37A*. This rule states that:

> A prisoner who is a party to any legal proceedings may correspond with his legal adviser in connection with the proceedings and unless the Governor has reason to suppose that any such correspondence contains matter not relating to the proceedings it shall not be read or stopped.

However the European Court of Human Rights held in 1992 that any examination of correspondence between a prisoner and his lawyer is a breach of his rights, which means inmates are entitled to seek advice or complain to a legal adviser about any aspect of their treatment in custody. Any incoming or outgoing letter may only be opened when the inmate is present, if prison staff strongly suspect it contains an illicit enclosure.

Any correspondence between inmates and a Member of Parliament, Member of the European Parliament, Consular and High Commission officials, the European Convention on Human Rights or the Criminal Cases Review Commission is treated as privileged and confidential.

A *special letter* is a first-class letter at public expense, which can be requested to correspond with a legal adviser or let visitors know of an impending transfer, by an inmate with no private cash. Category A prisoners are not forewarned about any moves, but prison staff will invite them to complete a form giving details of all visitors whom they wish to be advised of their whereabouts.

Foreign nationals who cannot receive their minimum entitlement of visits can ask for the cost of airmail postage to be paid instead.

Preventing problems with correspondence

A convicted prisoner is allowed to send out one letter a week at public expense. Generally there is no restriction on the number of letters that can be sent out at the inmate's own expense provided they can afford the postage from their earnings or private cash. However, inmates held in conditions of maximum security, or who are on the escape list, or whose mail is being routinely read, may find the Governor limits the number of letters they can send and restricts the length of outgoing letters to four sides of A5 paper. Further restrictions may be imposed for security reasons, if for example the volume of correspondence is excessive or the Governor has strong suspicions, or evidence, that the rules are being abused.

Prison Rule 33 gives wide discretionary powers to the Home Secretary to restrict communications. These are fully explained in Standing Order 5 which is in the prison library, or can be purchased by inmates and the general public.

The following restrictions apply to all outgoing correspondence:

* letters must not refer to an escape plan, or to anything that undermines the security of the prison, or that affects national security;
* they must not assist anyone to commit a criminal offence, including breaking Prison Rules;
* they must not contain threats of any sort, or be racially offensive or obscene.

Under the following circumstances an additional letter can be requested at public expense:

* communications with an outside probation officer or social worker;
* following conviction where it is necessary to sort out business problems;
* trying to resolve family or marital problems;
* searching for work or seeking accommodation on discharge.

Inmates may contribute to the letter pages of newspapers, write articles for publication, and participate in radio or television programmes provided they do not get paid. They cannot write about their own crime or the offences of other prisoners, and must not identify staff or other prisoners.

Permission is necessary if an inmate wishes to correspond with an inmate at another establishment, unless it is a close relative, or to their co-defendant about the trial or sentence imposed. Prior approval is necessary before writing to a victim or their family, and before placing an advertisement in a magazine or newspaper for a penfriend.

Letters can be written in any language but correspondence in a language other than English may be delayed if the Governor decides it has to be translated in order to be censored. In practice this is unlikely to occur in a low-security establishment.

Inmates who do not receive regular visits can ask for an extra letter instead.

Inmates are not prevented from writing to any close relatives, but if anyone writes formally to the Governor requesting that further letters are not sent, their wishes will be respected.

Inmates are allowed to receive stamped addressed envelopes in order to keep in contact with family and friends. This practice is based on one of the recommendations contained in the *Woolf Report* and does not form part of the Incentive and Earned Privileges Scheme; neither is it considered part of an inmate's private cash allowance.

In December 1998 measures were introduced to prevent any inmate who poses a risk to children from making contact with them. This applies to any inmate who has been charged with, or convicted of, offences against a child. Outgoing correspondence of any inmate remanded in custody or convicted of an offence under the Protection from Harassment Act 1997 will be routinely monitored.

RECEIVING VISITS

Maintaining contact and keeping relationships alive is of vital importance to anyone in prison. Visits play an important part in keeping families together, helping inmates keep in touch with the outside world and making preparations for their release.

The facilities and arrangements for visits vary considerably between different establishments. They can be significantly affected by factors such as overcrowding, staff shortages and the space available for visits.

The minimum entitlement for visits is laid down in Prison Rule 33 and Standing Order 5, which specifies that inmates should have one visit on first reception followed by visits of at least 30 minutes duration every two weeks. Visits do not normally occur on Good Fridays, Christmas Day and Bank Holidays.

Although the times and days vary, convicted inmates should be allowed a minimum of two 60-minute visits every four weeks, including one at the weekend.

Unconvicted prisoners are permitted a 15-minute visit every weekday. They should receive the equivalent of three hours of visits each week including one at the weekend lasting for at least half an hour.

In practice these standards are exceeded in many prisons and while there is no difference between male and female establishments, in Young Offender Institutions it is normal for visits to take place more frequently.

Making visiting arrangements

A visiting order is not necessary if visiting an unconvicted prisoner, but a visit to a convicted prisoner needs an official pass.

On first arrival inmates are issued with their first visiting order, which is known as a Reception VO. This is extra to the laid-down entitlement, but only valid for seven days. Inmates must specify on the visiting order who will be visiting, before sending it out. Normally three adults can be included on the visiting order in addition to their children, but they must all visit at the same time. All children visiting a convicted prisoner must be named on the visiting order. Visitors will only exceptionally be allowed to enter an establishment without a valid visiting order.

Any convicted inmates who have been identified as presenting a risk to children and who may attempt to pursue paedophiliac tendencies in custody are able to receive visits only from their own children and siblings.

Visiting orders (VO) are issued every fortnight but are only valid for 28 days. If a visitor cannot use a VO during that period a fresh one can only be issued if it is returned to the establishment.

In the case of a Category A prisoner, prospective visitors are subject to the Approved Visitors Scheme where they have to consent to security enquiries into their background. Once these are complete the visitor can be advised that normal visiting arrangements apply.

Most establishments have a Visitor Centre, run by volunteers, where visitors can wait and obtain light refreshments. There is usually a booking-in system so that formalities can be processed systematically, making it easier for visits to commence on time.

Before any visitors enter the visits room they are given a rub-down search. This is conducted by a member of staff of the same sex as the visitor, and consists of an examination of the outer clothing and hand baggage to ensure no unauthorised items are concealed. If prison staff suspect a visitor may be concealing contraband, a firearm or weapon, they will be asked to submit to a strip search, which is a more thorough search of all clothing. Prison staff are legally allowed to conduct such searches, but visitors have to give their consent and the search must be carried out considerately and in complete privacy. If the visitor refuses to be searched the staff can decline to allow the visit to take place or offer a *closed visit* as an alternative. Closed visits take place in a cubicle where no physical contact is possible.

Visitors to establishments with Category A prisoners are subject to an X-ray check in addition to a rub-down search. All hand baggage and coats are X-rayed and no personal items can be taken into the visits room, but will be locked in a secure locker until the visit has ended.

Meeting visiting needs

The visits area should be clean and tidy and include toilets, a canteen, a supervised children's play area, a baby changing area and access to a payphone. Most establishments have a creche or play area in the visits room where children can be supervised for short periods. A few prisons, notably HMP Holloway, Styal and Maidstone, have introduced arrangements where an inmate's children can visit for the whole day.

The aim is to enable visits to take place in a relaxed and informal atmosphere. This is not easily achieved in some establishments where closed circuit TV surveillance has proved necessary, or where the visits area has yet to be modernised.

Visitors are not allowed to give inmates anything during the visit apart from refreshments purchased from the prison canteen, and all food must be consumed during the visit. Unless the visits area is a No Smoking area, visitors may offer inmates cigarettes to smoke during the visit. In a Young Offender Institution smoking is normally prohibited or severely restricted.

If an inmate applies to have handed in, or hand out any personal property, including hobby items made in their cell or in classes, this will be dealt with by the officer in charge of visits.

Sentenced prisoners can decide to accumulate a minimum of three and a maximum of 24 visits, and apply to be temporarily transferred to an establishment nearer their family in order to receive visits. To be eligible for *accumulated visits* an inmate must wait until six months have elapsed since the move from the local prison. Currently overcrowding pressures are making this very difficult to arrange, but if a temporary transfer is approved it normally lasts for 28 days. Accumulated visits can be arranged every six months provided sufficient VOs have been saved up.

An *inter-prison visit* can be arranged if an inmate's close relative is also in prison. This can take place every three months provided both inmates agree to surrender a VO. Inter-prison visits can also be arranged for co-defendants held separately, to receive joint legal advice.

A solicitor or legal adviser has the right to visit inmates and speak to them confidentially, in sight but out of hearing of prison staff. They can visit at any reasonable time, although in practice it is sensible to book the use of the legal visits room in advance.

Other official visitors who require confidential facilities include the police, immigration officials, Inland Revenue inspectors, probation officers, social workers and staff from other government departments. Inmates may receive as many visits as necessary from their legal adviser or other official visitors as these do not count against the visiting allowance.

If an inmate's children are in the care of the local authority they can apply to see them under conditions where a degree of privacy is afforded. If those responsible for their care will not agree to this, arrangements can be made for them to be visited where they are being cared for, subject to a satisfactory risk assessment and staff availability. Visits to the child's home can take place every three months and do not count against an inmate's VO allowance.

Any inmate can ask to see the prison chaplain and request a Prison Visitor, that is, a local person who is willing to visit a prisoner who would not otherwise receive any visits.

Another option is to request visits from a voluntary associate. This is a volunteer who is willing to write to and visit inmates. The prison probation officer can put inmates in touch with voluntary associates, or they can make their own arrangements and write directly to New Bridge, an independent group of volunteers: New Bridge, 27a Medway Street, London SW1P 2BD.

USING THE TELEPHONE

On each wing there should be access to a telephone that takes the special phonecards produced for the Prison Service by British Telecom. These phonecards can only be obtained from the prison shop, but there is normally no limit on the number that can be purchased from earnings or private cash, irrespective of whether an inmate is convicted or unconvicted.

Access to the telephone is usually restricted under the Incentive and Earned Privilege System for those on the basic regime. No inmate in a Special Secure Unit (SSU) can have access to the telephone, and Category A and escape list prisoners have all calls monitored and recorded. The restrictions that apply to correspondence also apply to telephone conversations, and an offensive call, or one that poses a threat to the security, good order and discipline of the establishment would be disconnected. Telephone conversations of any inmate convicted and sentenced for an offence under the Protection from Harassment Act 1997 will be routinely monitored.

In an open prison calls are unrestricted, but random monitoring takes place in all other establishments. Once inmates have been advised that telephone monitoring takes place, under Section 2 of the Interception of Communications Act 1985, it means that if they use the telephones provided, they have automatically given consent for their calls to be monitored and tape recorded.

Inmates can apply to exchange a visiting order for a free telephone call if they are not receiving visits, but this is at the Governor's discretion. However, if there are compassionate grounds or an urgent need to contact a legal adviser, the Governor can authorise the use of an official telephone. Any approved call will be connected by a prison officer who will remain in the room for the duration of the call, unless it is to a legal adviser.

ATTENDING THE INDUCTION PROGRAMME

The day following reception into prison, inmates commence an induction programme. This is an opportunity to share information about the establishment and the standards of behaviour that are expected.

Information about the local routines, how to make applications and use of the Request and Complaints system are explained. Prisoners are advised who to approach for help with personal problems, advice on applying for bail, and obtaining legal aid to lodge an appeal.

Once sentenced, a date of release and parole eligibility date will be given to the prisoner. The time spent on the induction programme is an opportunity to assess an inmate's needs and abilities, as well as gauge suitability for a range of regime activities. A representative of the Education Department will carry out a needs analysis and conduct tests to assess any educational requirements. A member of the probation team will explain Throughcare, and information is provided by members of the Physical Education Department, the Chaplaincy team, the Medical Officer, the Industrial Manager or whoever is responsible for work allocation, and the Governor's representative.

Several practical issues will be resolved, including allocating a cell on a residential unit, providing letter-writing materials, explaining about access to the payphones, and offering guidance on how to safeguard existing employment and accommodation while in custody.

Inmates should be offered an opportunity to sign a prisoner's 'compact' which not only makes clear what is expected, but also sets out the benefits available under the Incentive and Earned Privilege Scheme in return for co-operating while in custody.

LOOKING FOR A RELEASE DATE

On 1 October 1992 the Criminal Justice Act 1991 came into effect, changing the rules about release dates for determinate sentenced prisoners.

Anyone sentenced before this date and still in custody will be released when two-thirds of their sentence has been completed; this is called the *earliest date of release* (EDR). However, inmates can be kept in prison until their *latest date of release* (LDR) if days have been added to their sentence for disciplinary offences.

Any qualifying time spent on remand, prior to being sentenced, counts towards the sentence. A High Court judgment in 1997, in the case of *McMahon*, confirmed the principle that remand time cannot be counted twice in situations where an inmate has two separate sentences passed at different times which shared a period of remand time.

Inmates may be eligible to be released on parole after one-third of the sentence has been completed, provided the Parole Board are satisfied that the risk is acceptable; this is called the *parole eligibility date* (PED). If parole is granted, supervision by the Probation Department lasts until the two-thirds point in the sentence has been reached. During the period of licence a discharged inmate can be recalled to prison if any of the parole licence conditions are broken.

After 1 October 1992 the position changed considerably:

- A sentence of less than 12 months brings automatic release at the halfway stage; this is called the *automatic release date* (ARD). Release is unconditional, known as *automatic unconditional release* (AUR) but inmates remain 'at risk' until their *sentence expiry date* (SED). If added days are awarded for disciplinary offences the prisoners can be kept in prison until the SED.
- A sentence of 12 months and over, but under four years, brings the *conditional release date* (CRD) at the halfway point. Conditional release, known as *automatic conditional release* (ACR), means release under supervision until three-quarters of the sentence is reached, known as the *licence expiry date* (LED), and inmates remain 'at risk' until their SED.
- A sentence of four years or more brings automatic release at the two-thirds stage of the sentence, known as the *non-parole date* (NPD), with supervision until three-quarters of the sentence is reached. Inmates can be considered for parole at the halfway stage of their sentence, known as the *parole eligibility date* (PED). If release on licence is approved, supervision lasts until three-quarters of the sentence is reached, except in the case of a sex offender where the trial judge can insist that supervision continues until the end of the sentence.
- *Discretionary conditional release* (DCR) applies to anyone serving over four years. In the case of those serving between four and seven years, the decision to grant parole will be taken by the Parole Board. Inmates serving over seven years will only be released subject to the approval of the Home Secretary on the recommendation of the Parole Board. Supervision continues until three-quarters of the sentence is reached in all such cases. For young offenders the position is slightly different. Everyone is supervised for a minimum of three months on release, or until their 22nd birthday, by a probation officer or social worker.

Anyone liable to be deported after his sentence is served will do so at the halfway stage if serving under four years; that is the ARD or CRD, whichever is applicable. If serving over four years, as soon as the halfway point in the sentence is reached (the PED), they will normally be deported. However, this can be delayed at the discretion of the Home Secretary until the two-thirds point in the sentence (the NPD).

UNDERSTANDING THE PAROLE SYSTEM

The Home Secretary has overall responsibility for all decisions concerning parole, but this task is delegated to the Parole Board.

The Home Secretary has issued clear instructions to the Parole Board:

In deciding whether or not to recommend release on licence, the Parole Board shall consider *primarily* the risk to the public of a further offence being committed at a time when the prisoner would otherwise be in prison and whether any such risk is acceptable.

The risk to the public of allowing release on licence has to be balanced against the possible benefits. The dilemma is whether releasing an offender back into society under minimal supervision will help with rehabilitation and reduce the likelihood of re-offending in the future, or whether it is safer, in the short term, to keep the offender in custody.

Before the Parole Board can reach a decision it must assess the risk to the public by considering the following points:

* The nature and circumstances of the original offence.
* Whether the behaviour and attitude displayed in custody demonstrates the offender is serious about addressing his offending behaviour.
* Is there is a greater risk of the inmate committing a violent or sexual offence than any other offence?
* Is he likely to conform with the conditions of parole licence?
* Will the longer period of supervision that parole provides reduce the risk of further offending?
* Has the supervising officer recommended any specific licence conditions?
* Has an effective resettlement plan been devised?

Parole is clearly seen as an integral part of the sentence management process. While the main purpose of sentence management is to prepare for a safer release, the main concern of the Parole Board is the risk to the public of a further offence.

The two aims are complementary. Sentence management can demonstrate to what extent an inmate has tackled his offending behaviour, which allows an ongoing assessment of the risks involved in releasing an individual on licence to be made.

CASE STUDIES

Rudd Basho worries about his pregnant girlfriend

Rudd Basho is a 17-year-old West Indian youngster whose girlfriend is both home-less and pregnant. It is his first sentence in a Young Offender Institution and he is very worried about how Lola will manage without him. He approaches his proba-tion officer and personal prison officer for help. His personal officer allows Rudd several special letters to write to the Social Services Department and the Housing Department about Lola's accommodation needs. Rudd makes an application to have an extra visit to advise and encourage her to make appointments with the Homeless Persons Unit, which is approved by the Wing Governor.

Peter Miles is placed on closed visits

Peter Miles is serving a five-year sentence for importing Class A drugs and is heavily involved in the prison drug scene. The Security Department believe his common-law wife is smuggling drugs in on visits, and Peter in turn is supplying other inmates. She is given a rub-down search on arrival and carefully monitored on closed circuit TV during the visit, and is observed discreetly passing a small package to Peter who hastily swallows the offending item when prison staff approach. The video evidence is later seen by the Governor who decides that Peter should be placed on closed visits; future visits take place in a cubicle where no physical contact is possible.

Paddy Naughtie joins the enhanced wages scheme

Paddy Naughtie has completed 15 years of a mandatory life sentence and his case has recently been formally reviewed by the Parole Board. He is expecting to be transferred to a lower security prison and in the meantime has progressed to the enhanced regime. He has been selected to work in a new workshop undertaking work for a private company and qualifies for the enhanced wages scheme. His current earnings average £7 per week but with performance pay and productivity bonuses he expects to earn £20 per week, of which £4 will be saved for his eventual discharge.

Nicola Harrington requests a Prison Visitor

Nicola Harrington is six months pregnant and is serving her second custodial sen-tence. She is separated from her violent, drug-dependent boyfriend, and feels all alone as she has few friends and no family alive in this country. The prison proba-tion officer offers to put her in touch with a voluntary associate, but she decides to write to New Bridge and make her own arrangements. At her request the prison chaplain arranges for her to receive visits from a local woman with a young family who has been appointed a Prison Visitor, and she starts visiting Nicola on a regular basis.

CHECKLIST

- How much property can be kept in a cell?
- Why would a special letter be requested?
- When will correspondence be read by staff?
- How much private cash can an unconvicted prisoner spend?
- What is the minimum wage a sentenced prisoner must receive?
- Can visitors be searched by prison staff?
- Who qualifies for parole?

- Which prisoners are placed on the basic regime?
- How can an appellant benefit from Prison Rule 37A?
- When would the Governor prevent an inmate from writing to a close relative?
- What are closed visits?
- Which prisoners remain 'at risk' until their sentence expiry date?

- When can a prisoner qualify for the enhanced earning scheme?
- How does a prisoner qualify for accumulated visits?
- What is a Prison Visitor?
- When do prison staff monitor telephone calls?
- Which prisoners have a discretionary release date?

DISCUSSION POINTS

1. Examine the advantages and disadvantages of prisoners being allowed to have their own television sets in their cells.

2. 'Allowing prisoners to spend private cash penalises those who are poorer and acts as a disincentive to work.' Discuss.

3. The introduction of volumetric control penalises all prisoners and conflicts with the spirit behind the Incentive and Earned Privilege System. How can the correct balance be struck between security considerations and rewarding good behaviour?

4. 'The distinction between prisoners serving under 12 months, those serving between 12 months and under four years, and those serving longer sentences is arbitrary and over-complicated.' Discuss.

5. Would the system for releasing prisoners on licence be improved if the Parole Board were independent of political control?

6. Examine the advantages and disadvantages of allowing conjugal visits to take place in penal establishments.

CHAPTER 3

Sentence Management

CONTRIBUTING TO THE
SENTENCE MANAGEMENT PROCESS

The National Framework for the Throughcare of Offenders agreed jointly by the Prison and Probation Services is a commitment by both services to work together to devise and deliver programmes aimed at addressing and reducing offending behaviour. The overall aim is to devise a sentence plan which takes account of both the custodial and supervisory parts of the sentence. It should tackle some of an inmate's identified needs in prison and decide which should be dealt with during the supervisory part of the sentence.

As a result, the Sentence Planning process was revised and re-launched in 1997 as *Sentence Management* in order to:

- develop an approach which reduces the likelihood of further offending and a subsequent return to prison;
- assist inmates make the best use of their time in custody;
- devise a successful plan to resettle back into the community;
- counter meanwhile the harmful effects of being imprisoned;
- provide continuity when inmates have to transfer to another establishment during their sentence.

Once the initial assessment, categorisation and allocation procedures have been completed, the intention is to gather together all the available information and use it to predict and assess risks more accurately. An additional aim is to provide an appropriate regime and range of programmes which relate to these identified needs.

There are several stages to the Sentence Management process:

1. the categorisation of juveniles, male and female young offenders (YOs) and male and female adults;
2. the preparation of an initial sentence plan for Category A prisoners and the sentence plan for all other prisoners;
3. the sentence plan review, which reviews the security category and the appropriateness of the establishment where the inmates is currently serving his sentence;
4. the risks involved in approving release on temporary licence;

5. the preparation of a parole assessment;
6. the preparation of pre-discharge and discharge reports;
7. release on licence under supervision so that it becomes a seamless sentence.

The sentence management process is intended to be as effective as possible with supervising and seconded probation officers maintaining a close liaison with prison staff and exchanging information.

CONTACT WITH VICTIMS

The Probation Service has a responsibility to contact the victims of serious violence or a sexual offence within two months of the sentence being passed. Under the Victim's Charter 1996 they are obliged to provide the victim and their family with information about the custodial process and their rights to be consulted when parole or temporary release is being considered. While victims are not entitled to be given personal information about inmates, in order to guard against possible retaliation, they have a right to express their concerns and have their views taken into account when the time comes to decide what licence conditions should apply.

Understandably there are limits to openness, as the wishes and rights of the victim to privacy must be respected. This is similar to the right of inmates not to have medical information entered on their sentence planning documents without permission. Victims have a right to refuse to have their concerns disclosed to the inmate and they are entitled to read that part of the parole assessment that represents their views.

Any written assessments by staff on inmates must be disclosed to them; the only exceptions are:

- if national security is involved;
- in order to prevent a crime being committed or a breach of security from occurring;
- to protect the interests of victims;
- on the grounds of medical confidentiality or for psychiatric reasons.

ADDRESSING NEEDS

The individual circumstances and identifiable needs of inmates should be handled with understanding and sensitivity.

A physical disability that affects mobility, problems of visual impairment, hearing difficulties, a learning difficulty or disability (commonly known as a mental handicap) call for skilled professional help.

It is easy for certain exhibited behaviour to be misinterpreted. An inmate with special needs expressing frustration can be perceived as a show of aggression. Others with mental health problems, degenerative conditions, the elderly, ethnic minority groups and prisoners who are themselves victims need skilled assistance.

Foreign nationals face particular problems which can easily make them feel isolated and anxious about their circumstances, particularly if there is a language difficulty. Efforts should be made to keep foreign nationals together and priority given to providing an interpreter and an opportunity for English tuition. The Race Relations Liaison Officer, chaplain or the seconded probation team should have access to community-based workers who can provide support and advice.

The sentence management process will only be successful if inmates are fully involved and their needs carefully addressed. The resulting plan should give priority to issues which are likely to reduce the risk of re-offending.

The focus of sentence management for young offenders of either sex, irrespective of whether they have only a matter of weeks left to serve, will be on their resettlement plans.

The main priority will be to ensure:

- they have a suitable address to go to on release;
- there is contact with the Social Services Department or Probation Service who will provide supervision on release;
- they are not a child protection case;
- they do not pose a danger to the public.

All targets set must be *SMART*, that is Specific, Measurable, Achievable, Realistic and Time-bounded.

Some targets will be achievable in the short term, some in the longer term. Others may not be achievable. Certain needs will not be able to be met. Expectations of all concerned need to be realistic, otherwise disenchantment will set in. Resources are finite and under considerable pressure.

SECURITY REVIEWS

Everyone serving more than 12 months will have their security category reviewed regularly and also whenever a significant change in circumstances occurs or there is a clear change in the risk factor; in time inmates are normally downgraded.

This review process will happen several times during a lifer's sentence. Before they can eventually be released they will be tested in open conditions. The progress of each lifer is considered by the Lifer Management Unit in Headquarters, and the first review held within 12 months of the date of sentence.

Similarly, all Category A inmates' security categorisation is reviewed by the 'Category A Committee' on an annual basis.

PREDICTING RISKS

Assessing and predicting risks is fundamental to the whole concept of sentence management. The purpose of carrying out risk assessments is:

- to identify relevant factors that affect the level of risk an inmate poses;
- to reduce the risk level and attempt to predict the future risk;
- to provide information which assists correct decisions to be reached during the custodial part of the sentence and when released on licence;

- to make the best use of all the available resources, such as accredited offender treatment programmes.

While it is appreciated the risk element changes over time as circumstances and situations alter, the risks that are of concern to both the prison authorities and probation service are as follows:

- the protection of the public;
- the risk of violent offences;
- the risk of sexual offences;
- the risk of other offences occurring;
- the risk of substance abuse;
- the risks to other prisoners and staff;
- the risk of escape or absconding;
- the risk of control problems arising;
- the risk of inmates coming under pressure, being bullied and finding themselves unable to cope;
- the risk of suicide or self-harm.

Research indicates it is more useful to identify potentially harmful behaviour than attempting to predict which offenders are likely to be dangerous.

Using this evidence the Prison Service has developed a computer-based risk predictor which draws on the histories and re-offending patterns of 40,000 prisoners. The risk predictor assesses the following:

- the likelihood of a further custodial sentence;
- the risk of committing a violent offence;
- the risk of a sexual offence occurring;
- the likelihood of any other offending behaviour re-occurring.

This programme has been introduced into every prison and a risk prediction can be made if the following information is fed into the computer:

- details of gender and age;
- the length of the current sentence;
- the inmate's age when first convicted ;
- the number of previous custodial sentences served under the age of 21 and the number of sentences subsequently served;
- full details of any previous convictions including all violent or sexual offences;
- full details of the current offence.

Once this information has been correctly programmed into the computer, the risk predictor scales can indicate the likelihood of the following events occurring:

- the likelihood of an inmate being imprisoned for a violent offence within two years of release;
- a reconviction for a sexual offence within two years of release;
- a reconviction for any offence within two years of release;
- the risk of an inmate being imprisoned for any offence within two years of discharge.

Once the risk predictor scores are printed out they become part of the sentence planning documentation. Inmates are then placed into one of four groups depending on the risk they pose of re-offending within two years. These predictions are discussed with inmates, particularly those who fall into the two higher categories of risk, who are invited to examine how they can avoid returning to custody in the future.

The idea is to encourage inmates to think carefully about how they intend to address their offending behaviour, particularly if they are serious about trying to persuade the Parole Board to release them early on licence.

RECONVICTION RATES

The likelihood of reconviction can be assessed using the risk predictor, which is based on the historical pattern of offending of prisoners who have been released with similar offending records, who re-offend within two years of release.

The following examples of Risk Prediction for Sentence Management need to be interpreted in the following way:

- *Risk of reconviction for violent offending or reconviction for sexual offending*
  either:
  > No history.
  > Some.
  > Raised.
  > High.
- *Risk of reconviction for other offending or re-imprisonment*
  either:
  > Low.
  > Low medium.
  > High medium.
  > High.

The statistical evidence that an inmate will be reconvicted for a violent offence within two years, resulting in imprisonment, is as follows:

No History	No recorded convictions for violence.
Some	At least one previous conviction for a violent offence.
Raised	About four times the risk of those in the *same* category.
High	About nine times the risk of those in the *same* category.

The risk of being reconvicted of a sexual offence within two years is as follows:

No History   No recorded convictions for sexual offences.
Some   At least one previous conviction for a sexual offence.
Raised   About four times the risk of those in the *same* category.
High   About thirty times the risk of those in the *same* category.

The risk of being reconvicted of other offending within two years of release is as follows:

Low   About 15 in 100 will be reconvicted within two years.
Low medium   About 35 in 100 will be reconvicted within two years.
High medium About 65 in 100 will be reconvicted within two years.
High   About 85 in 100 will be reconvicted within two years.

The risk of reimprisonment reflects the likelihood of an inmate being reconvicted of an offence, for which they would receive a custodial offence within two years of their release from prison, and is as follows:

Low   About 5 in 100.
Low medium   About 15 in 100.
High medium About 35 in 100.
High   About 60 in 100.

PREVENTING SUICIDE AND SELF-HARM

Assessing the risk of suicide or self-harm is part of the sentence management process.

The risk of self-harm occurring is greatest when an inmate is first received into custody, whenever their status changes, for instance when they are sentenced, and after a move to a new establishment. It is difficult to tell how someone is feeling unless they tell a member of staff or another inmate. Discussing their suicidal feelings and worries helps an anxious inmate to take control of the situation that is defeating them.

Prison staff will be concerned to find out how somebody is coping if it is their first time in custody or they have previously felt suicidal. Other signals that raise concern are previous contact with psychiatric services, a family history of self-harm, a history of drug or alcohol abuse, evidence of being bullied, anxieties about a long custodial sentence and excessive guilt over an offence of sex or violence. If any of these factors is present and there is evidence of a lack of any positive hope for the future, possibly because parole has been refused or they have received a letter ending a relationship, then staff need to treat them as warning signs and be alert to the possibility that a vulnerable individual may contemplate self-injury or suicide.

There can be additional pressures on female inmates caused by the onset of the menopause, pre-menstrual and post-natal depression, pregnancy, abortion, and the pain of separation from their children. All these are stressful events that can trigger suicidal feelings.

A young offender may feel vulnerable in the early stages of his sentence or while on remand. Youngsters are more likely to make an impulsive suicidal attempt if they have self-injured previously and are experiencing problems coping with imprisonment.

Adults are more likely to consider suicide as an option if their offence is very serious and they have a history of psychiatric problems.

Past experience suggests there are three main types of inmate who commit suicide while in custody:

1   those *poor at coping;*
2   *long-term prisoners* facing serious charges;
3   the *mentally ill.*

- Those who have difficulty coping are normally the younger element with a history of self-harm. Often abused as children, they face problems coping with the stress of being in custody.
- Those serving a lengthy sentence for serious charges involving sex and violence are more at risk when on remand, particularly if facing a life sentence. They often find that family problems, bereavements and parole knockbacks are particularly stressful. These events can act as the trigger for a well-planned and determined suicide attempt to be made, usually at night.
- If an inmate is suffering from a recognised mental illness like a serious depressive illness, a psychopathic or personality disorder, or a psychotic illness, then they are potentially at high risk. Often the illness is related to drug and alcohol abuse, they are socially isolated, and feeling vulnerable.

Fortunately a severe suicidal crisis is generally short-lived. The risks can be significantly reduced if continuous support and supervision is available during the initial 24-hour period. The priority is for emotional support in the early stages, and anyone who offers friendship and caring support can literally be a lifesaver.

Once the initial crisis is over, consideration can be given to tackling the underlying problems. Needs can range from practical help, medical attention, ongoing befriending, offering advice with family problems, to providing a range of specialised therapeutic services. This can include individual counselling, groupwork, or involvement in psychological programmes based on behavioural principles.

Identifying those at risk

In 1994 the Prison Service developed a strategy of 'Caring for the Suicidal' which reduces the likelihood of suicide and self-harm incidents from occurring in the following ways:

- *Primary care*
  This involves creating a safe environment and helping inmates cope with being in custody by providing a range of counselling and welfare services geared to meeting their particular needs. This includes making sure that inmates have the opportunity to contact the Samaritans whenever necessary.

- *Special care*
  This involves conducting an assessment on reception to identify anyone in crisis who is possibly 'at risk'. If staff are concerned that an inmate is not coping they complete a *Self Harm at Risk Form* (F2052SH) and take it to the Health Care Centre. This alerts medical staff who can decide whether to move the inmate into shared or supervised accommodation. They may decide to provide in-patient support by admitting an individual temporarily to the prison hospital and keeping them under observation until the crisis is over. These precautions also apply to Category A prisoners and those on the Escape List, who can be allocated shared accommodation under certain circumstances.
- *Aftercare*
  This means catering for the inmate's needs once the crisis is over, helping them to make a full recovery and improving their ability to cope by making sure they receive the necessary help and support to address underlying problems.
- *Community responsibility*
  This means recognising everyone has a part to play, staff and inmates alike. *The Chief Inspectors' Report on Suicide and Self-harm* recommends that prisoners accept some responsibility for each other's welfare and become actively involved in suicide prevention.

Each establishment is expected to conduct a health screening on everyone received from the courts or transferred from another prison or Young Offender Institution. On reception, inmates should be offered support and help, particularly if they have previously tried to harm themselves or are considered to be at risk of suicide or self-harm.

Each establishment should have a Suicide Awareness Team or Co-ordinator with responsibility for monitoring the strategy and local arrangements. Their role includes identifying suitable inmates who can befriend other 'at-risk' prisoners, or who are willing to become trained as *listeners*.

The Samaritans

The Prison Service work closely with the Samaritans in order to care and support anyone who feels suicidal while in custody. They are available 24 hours a day for crisis intervention, and recently launched a national number: 0345 90 90 90.

On dialling this number callers are put through to the nearest Samaritan centre and only charged for the call at the local rate.

The Samaritans' *Outreach Programme* is an initiative designed to make their services more accessible to those in residential care or hospital who cannot call their centres. In 1994 they set up a new Prison Support Team in order to offer advice, support and a befriending service to those in custody.

In each establishment it should be possible for everyone to have access to the Samaritans at any time during the day, particularly anyone experiencing a serious crisis. All contact between Samaritans and callers is strictly confidential; telephone calls are not monitored, and neither are letters read.

Some establishments, including HMP Swansea, Deerbolt and Bedford, have a direct line to the local Samaritan branch from the Health Care Centre. Others like HMP

Exeter, Standford Hill, Gloucester, Shrewsbury, Nottingham, The Verne and Brinsford have special extensions on the wing which are programmed to connect with the local Samaritan branch. An extra official telephone where privacy can be guaranteed and which is dedicated for calls to the Samaritans is provided at HMP Lincoln, Ford, Werrington, Cookham Wood and Bristol. At HMYOI Lancaster Farms and Feltham access is provided to a mobile telephone.

The Samaritans develop and support prisoner befriending schemes or 'Listener Schemes', which currently cover around 80 establishments and operate in line with Samaritan principles. Potential listeners are usually identified by prison staff who then refer them for assessment and training to the Samaritans. This training stresses the importance of confidentiality and encourages listeners to help anyone feeling suicidal or in distress to seek help from staff. Any inmates who feel they could be a listener and offer help and support to others in need, should be encouraged to express interest to prison staff.

ABUSING DRUGS

Many inmates told the Learmont Inquiry Team that drugs are the root cause of many problems in prison.

The most usual route for drugs to enter an establishment is on social visits. Their availability causes concern to many inmates because the level of intimidation, bullying and assaults often has a direct link with drug abuse. Drug users put pressure on their visitors and those temporarily released on licence to smuggle in drugs to keep their habit going. Often users build up debts with their suppliers. When this occurs repaying these favours may mean getting involved in carrying out assaults on other prisoners or applying pressure on their families, in order to pay off their debts.

The Learmont Inquiry Report highlighted how phonecards are regularly used as currency to purchase drugs, for gambling, for trading or to pay off debts. At HMP Parkhurst, inmates at the bottom of the pecking order had to pay the barons phonecards to go on the landing for association.

The Report of an Inquiry by Her Majesty's Chief Inspector of Prisons into The Disturbance at HMP Wymott on 6th September 1993 found evidence of bullying, intimidation, regular assaults, widespread vandalism, a gangland culture and drug problems. Drug-taking was undermining the regime and threatening the safety of other inmates. Both the Chief Inspector of Prisons and the Learmont report recommended the introduction of drug-free wings, drug testing, and drug awareness programmes, to educate, inform and help those wanting to combat the habit. Drug-free wings and mandatory drug testing offers some protection, particularly to those afraid of becoming a victim of the drug culture, and may help to isolate those who gain power from drug trafficking.

Sharing needles is a high-risk strategy and a certain recipe for infection or contracting HIV. During the Learmont Inquiry some inmates told the enquiry team they had seen over 40 people sharing the same needle.

Combating drug taking is in everyone's interests. The following measures are used to prevent drugs coming into establishments on social visits:

- the random searching of visitors;
- providing lockers for visitors' hand luggage;
- installing closed circuit TV (CCTV) in the visits area;
- intelligence-gathering systems based on Security Information Reports (SIRs) from staff;
- strip searching inmates after each visit;
- placing inmates involved in trafficking incidents on closed visits;
- carrying out compulsory drug testing;
- making greater use of sniffer dogs.

There are several ways of helping inmates experiencing drug problems:

- health education and drug awareness classes, which highlight the dangers of drug misuse;
- self-help groups which support those committed to abstinence;
- offering advice and support by means of individual or group counselling;
- providing treatment programmes on a modular basis at drug rehabilitation units or in long-term therapeutic communities;
- using the knowledge and resources of specialist voluntary groups;
- obtaining advice and information from the Local Health Authority and Social Services Department.

Tackling drugs in prison

In May 1998 the Prison Service launched a new drug strategy called 'Tackling Drugs in Prison' which complements the Government's national ten-year strategy 'Tackling Drugs to Build a Better Britain'.

The aims of this policy, which are constructed around the four aims contained in 'Tackling Drugs in Prison', are as follows:

1. *To help young people resist drug misuse in order to achieve their full potential in society*
   (a) to control the supply and demand for drugs in custody;
   (b) to develop best practice in education about drug misuse, given that the peak age for drug misuse amongst prisoners is 23;
   (c) to provide effective throughcare for juveniles and young offenders on release;
   (d) to examine the particular needs of female prisoners.
2. *To protect our communities from drug-related anti-social and criminal behaviour*
   (a) to develop a performance indicator in prisons which measures the effectiveness of the Governor's action against suppliers and dealers;
   (b) by using the Incentive and Earned Privilege System to reward drug-free behaviour;
   (c) by encouraging Governors to discriminate effectively within the disciplinary system between more and less harmful drug-related activity;
   (d) by conducting research to assess the effectiveness of prison-based intervention strategies.

3. *To enable people with drug problems to overcome them and live healthy and crime-free lives*
   (a) To appoint Area Drug Co-ordinators to conduct a needs analysis in each area and develop strategies to give all prisoners access to voluntary testing;
   (b) to reduce the number of random drug tests in order to target persistent offenders and carry out more voluntary testing on those who are determined to address their drug habit;
   (c) to tackle drug issues in the sentence management process and provide more effective treatment and throughcare arrangements.
4. *To shift the availability of illegal drugs on our streets*
   (a) to share best practice around the Prison Service;
   (b) to disrupt the prisoner's networks for distributing illegal drugs in prisons;
   (c) to reward drug-free behaviour through the Incentives and Earned Privilege System.

This range of measures will be complemented by continuing action to reduce the supply of drugs in prisons by:

* searching prisoners and their visitors;
* making improvements to perimeter security;
* the increased use of CCTV;
* using active and passive drug dogs;
* taking action against visitors who are involved in drug-related offences at establishments. During 1997 a total of 1176 visitors were arrested.

Mandatory drug testing

The *Criminal Justice and Public Order Act 1994* amended the Prison Act 1952 by adding Section 16A. This introduced mandatory drug testing to discourage the use of illicit drugs in prison. It is a disciplinary offence under Prison Rule 47 paragraph 8A to 'administer a controlled drug to himself or fail to prevent the administration of a controlled drug to him by another person'.

The Prison Service has made it clear it will not tolerate the use of drugs in prison and will do everything possible to reduce the availability and demand for drugs. It intends to try to educate, advise and treat anyone who has a drug problem.

Inmates are required to provide a urine sample for the purpose of drug testing under the following circumstances:

* *Risk assessment*
  Anyone being considered for a position of trust on an outside work party, or for release on temporary licence.
* *On reception*
  Whenever inmates return from a period of release on temporary licence, on first admission, or on transfer to the establishment. Disciplinary action is not taken against anyone on first reception as any drug detected will have been taken before they came into custody.

- *On reasonable suspicion*
  If prison staff have reasonable grounds to suspect someone is taking drugs.
- *The frequent test programme*
  Anyone found guilty of a drug-related offence in custody on more than one occasion is liable to be placed on the frequent testing programme and expected to provide a sample on a regular basis.
- *Random testing*
  An inmate's name may be selected on a totally random basis by computer for drug testing. Each month 10 per cent of the population are tested in this way.

Once an inmate has been selected for drug testing he is taken to the drug testing centre and required to provide a urine sample. He is given a maximum of five hours to produce a sample. This sample is sent to a laboratory for analysis together with full details of any medication currently being taken by the inmate. Refusal to provide a sample within the time limit results in a disciplinary charge under Rule 47 paragraph 19 for 'disobeying a lawful order'. Once proved the punishment is likely to be similar to that of testing positive.

The length of time drugs remain in the body varies, depending on the drug taken, the frequency of use and the individual's metabolism. The following are the minimum periods illicit drugs remain in the body:

amphetamines including methamphetamines	4 days
barbiturates, except phenobarbital	5 days
phenobarbital	30 days
benzodiazepines	30 days
cannabis, light use, once or twice each week	10 days
heavy use, daily	30 days
cocaine	4 days
methadone	5 days
LSD	3 days
opiates including morphine and codeine	5 days

Inmates required to give a urine sample are given a *Mandatory Drug Test Authorisation Form* (see p. 162). This explains why they have been asked for a sample, advises them of the laid-down procedure, and seeks their permission for details of any medication currently being taken.

A copy of the *Prison Service Chain of Custody Procedure* (see p. 163) is handed to each person being tested, which must be followed precisely if the tests are to be valid. The inmate is then asked to verify that:

- the reason for requesting a sample was explained to them;
- the sample provided was their own;
- the sample was divided, and sealed in their presence.

The seals used on the sample bottles carry a barcode that is identical to the barcode attached to the chain of custody form.

Two different tests can be carried out on the urine sample. The first laboratory test, known as the *screening test*, is generally reliable but can under certain circumstances react with other drugs present in the sample to give a misleading result. Once the test results have been returned to the establishment and the effect of any prescribed medication assessed, the inmate is informed. If the result is positive they are placed on a disciplinary charge. If a plea of not guilty is entered, the hearing will be adjourned for a more elaborate *confirmation test* to be made. This test is very accurate, and acts as a double check to guard against any possibility of human error. Once the results of the confirmation test are known, the disciplinary hearing can resume.

Dangerous drugs

A wide range of drugs are readily available in society and are more accessible than ever before. Inevitably illicit drugs find their way into prisons and Young Offender Institutions, but the dangers of taking drugs in custody are considerable.

The spread of **hepatitis B**, and the **Human Immunodeficiency Virus** (HIV) has as much to do with having unprotected sex as sharing drug-injecting equipment. Apart from the problem of obtaining an unadulterated supply, the risks range from the side-effects of the illicit substances themselves, to the possibility of serving additional days in custody following a positive drug test.

The **opioides** group of drugs includes heroin, codeine, opium, buprenorphine, dipipanone, pethidine, dextromoramide, dextropropoxyphene, dihydrocodeine, morphine and methadone.

Heroin, or diacetylmorphine or diamorphine, is a Class A drug used by medical practitioners for severe pain control such as that experienced by terminally ill patients. Heroin is a white powder, referred to as 'H', 'smack', 'junk', or 'skag', which can be taken orally, sniffed, smoked and injected. It is highly addictive and carries with it the risk of infection from HIV/AIDS, septiceamia and hepatitis if drug users share a needle. They also run the risk of killing themselves if there are impurities in the injected heroin. Anyone who is pregnant and addicted to heroin will be maintained on a low dose of opiates until after the birth, as sudden withdrawal can kill the unborn foetus.

Barbiturates, **benzodiazepines** and **solvents** all depress the nervous system and make the user feel relaxed and sociable. It is very easy to overdose on barbiturates, as the lethal dose is close to the normal dose. Barbiturates are a Class B drug, which comes in tablet or capsule form and is used for the treatment of severe insomnia and epilepsy.

Benzodiazepines are a Class C drug and are the most commonly prescribed drug in Britain. They include chlorodiazepoxide, Lorazepam and Diazepam, but are more commonly known as Valium, Librium, Ativan, Mogadon and Serenid. They have a similar effect to tranquillisers but can produce excessive emotional responses, aggression and unusual behaviour.

The term **solvents** covers glue, contact adhesive, nail varnish, lighter fuel, cleaning fluid, correcting fluid and the propellant gases in aerosols and fire extinguishers. The effect of solvent abuse on the user is similar to that of being drunk, and common side-effects are slurred speech, double vision and nausea. The risks include the possibility of heart failure, and suffocation due to the use of plastic bags. The gases in aerosols can cause sudden swelling to occur resulting in blocked airways, which causes rapid suffocation. Those who sniff in groups often experience hallucinations, and risk injury or worse if they lose control while under the influence.

Amphetamines are a Class B drug which stimulate the nervous system, increasing energy levels and reducing the need for sleep. Commonly known as 'speed', 'uppers', 'whizz', 'rit' and 'dexies' it is a crystalline powder available in pills, capsules and injectable form. If used to excess it can cause strokes, delusions, hallucinations, paranoia, violent behaviour and psychological dependence.

Cocaine is a Class A drug which induces an initial euphoria, later replaced by nausea, paranoia and restlessness. Known as 'coke', 'snow', 'ice', 'freebase' and 'crack', it is an odourless white crystalline powder, which can be sniffed or snorted through a tube, and injected. Users of cocaine may experience heart problems, digestive disorders, nasal damage and lose their libido.

Hallucinogens come in a variety of forms. Hallucinogenic amphetamines are Class A drugs which increase the user's confidence leaving them with a sense of euphoria. Commonly known as 'Ecstasy', 'E', 'XTC', 'Adam', 'Eve', 'disco biscuits', 'love doves', 'New Yorkers', 'disco burgers', 'phase 4' and 'phase 7', they come in tablets or capsules. Those who take hallucinogens may experience nausea, depression, paranoia and feel extremely anxious. They are particularly hazardous to those who suffer with epilepsy, diabetes, heart problems, hypertension, or are pregnant. Women users are also inclined to get infections of the genito-urinary tract.

Hallucinogenic mushrooms are Class A drugs with similar properties to amphetamines. Known as 'liberty cap', 'magic mushrooms', and 'fly agaric', they are eaten fresh, cooked or made into a drink.

Synthetic hallucinogens are Class A drugs which create mood changes and flashbacks often up to several weeks later. They are commonly referred to as 'LSD', 'acid', 'dots', and 'angel dust'. They are a synthetic white powder which is made into tablets or capsules and absorbed on to paper, gelatine sheets and sugar cubes. They can be smoked, sniffed, injected or simply taken with food or drink. The side-effects are disorientation, anxiety states and paranoia.

Cannabis is a Class B drug, which acts as a mild sedative, relaxes and reduces inhibitions. It is known by a variety of names including 'pot', 'blow', 'dope', 'draw', 'grass', 'weed', 'hash' or 'hashish', 'oil' and 'honey'. It is usually smoked, but can be eaten or made into a drink. Doctors use it to counteract the nausea that is associated with chemotherapy. It can cause respiratory problems, as it has three times the tar content of ordinary tobacco and the inhaled smoke stays in the body for longer.

Some over-the-counter medicines prescribed for colds, flu and diarrhoea can have opiate-like effects. Medicines like codeine, when once in the body convert 10 per cent of the drug into morphine. Taking a large quantity in order to get the desired effect runs the risk of paracetamol poisoning. Medicines such as Benylin, Night Nurse and Contact 400 can produce a sedative-like effect, whilst products like Day Nurse, diet pills and laxatives can produce effects similar to stimulants.

AVOIDING HIV/AIDS

Acquired Immune Deficiency Syndrome (AIDS), is caused by a virus called HIV. Anyone anxious about the risk of HIV/AIDS can seek confidential advice and treatment. Testing for HIV is entirely voluntary and free of charge, and those requesting a test are offered counselling by trained staff.

The HIV virus cannot be passed on to anyone through normal social contact. Individuals are only at risk if blood or semen from an HIV-positive person enters their bloodstream. This can happen if there is an exchange of bodily fluids, such as occurs if you have vaginal or anal sexual intercourse with someone who is infected. Sharing needles or syringes to inject drugs is the other main danger, and tattooing can be equally hazardous. The safest assumption to make in custody, is that everyone is potentially HIV-positive. Those about to be discharged or being released on temporary licence can request a small supply of condoms from the Health Care Centre free of charge.

Currently there is no known cure for AIDS, neither is there a vaccine to offer protection against it. Fortunately, not everyone who is HIV-positive develops AIDS. Anyone who has a test carried out which proves to be positive will be offered regular help to prevent or delay a HIV-related disease from developing. Their condition will be regularly reviewed every three months, even if no symptoms are evident. Someone who is HIV-positive and displaying symptoms will be reviewed on a regular basis and all necessary steps taken to provide them with appropriate respite or terminal care, and early release on compassionate medical grounds may be considered.

CASE STUDIES

Rudd Basho has difficulty coping with custody

Rudd Basho is serving his first custodial sentence and is very worried about Lola, his pregnant girlfriend who is homeless. The Social Services Department offered to provide care for the baby, but the Housing Department are unwilling to treat her as a homeless person. Rudd is finding everything is more than he can cope with; to make matters worse, he cannot obtain a place on the Motor Mechanics Course, and another youngster is bullying him. He confides in his personal officer, who makes a 'Self-Harm at Risk' referral. A case discussion takes place, and it is decided Rudd would benefit from a move to a shared cell. A mature and sympathetic youngster befriends him and staff carefully monitor the situation. A week later Rudd appears to be coping much better with life in custody.

Peter Miles is dealing in illicit drugs

Peter Miles is placed on closed visits after his common-law wife is observed on the closed circuit TV cameras on visits, passing a small package to him, which he promptly swallowed. Peter is suspected by staff of dealing in drugs. There are security reports of him strong-arming known drug users and acquiring a large supply of phonecards which he is using as currency. A full search of his cell is carried out and he is strip searched and given a mandatory drug test on the grounds of reasonable suspicion. The test proves positive and he is charged with a disciplinary offence. He pleads guilty and the charge is proved. Following the adjudication the Governor places him on the frequent testing programme.

Paddy Naughtie is tested for HIV

Paddy Naughtie is serving a life sentence and is making good progress. He has been told he will shortly be moving to an open prison and is starting to make plans for a new life on release. He gave up any involvement in the drug scene months earlier, but is worried that as he shared a needle with another prisoner still heavily involved in the drug scene, he may have the HIV virus. He requests an HIV test from the Medical Officer and is relieved to learn he is completely clear.

Nicola Harrington has a random drug test

Nicola Harrington has been selected by computer for random testing. She is taken to the drug testing centre and asked to provide a sample. She is abusive and uncooperative, but eventually provides a sample which is sent away for testing. The initial screening test proves positive, and she is charged under Prison Rule 47(A). Nicola pleads not guilty and insists she has not been taking cannabis as alleged. The hearing is adjourned for a confirmation test to be carried out at the laboratory and this confirms the presence of cannabinoids. The hearing resumes and she is found guilty as charged.

CHECKLIST

- What is a risk assessment?
- How do the rights of the victims of serious crime affect a prisoner?
- What is a listener scheme?
- When are the risks of suicide or self-harm greatest?
- What are the dangers of sharing drug-injecting equipment?

- How often is a security category reviewed?
- Who makes contributions to the sentence plan?
- How can prisoners contact the Samaritans?
- What criteria are used to place prisoners on the frequent testing programme?
- Why is it a disciplinary offence to fail to provide a urine sample?
- How are prisoners selected for random drug testing?

- What is meant by a community responsibility in relation to the strategy of 'Caring for the Suicidal?'
- How do staff assess the likelihood of a prisoner being reconvicted?
- What are the main aims of the drug strategy 'Tackling Drugs in Prison'?
- Why do prisoners believe drugs cause many problems in prisons?
- Why are hallucinogens and opioides hazardous for women?
- In what ways can cannabis be detrimental to health?

DISCUSSION POINTS

1. Examine the advantages and disadvantages of extending the Victim's Charter to cover all offences.

2. 'The notion of using a Risk Predictor as a tool to assess future behaviour and in particular the likelihood of reconviction is fundamentally flawed.' Discuss.

3. Has the abolition of routine censoring of mail increased the risk of suicide and self-harm for vulnerable prisoners?

4. Examine current practice critically and suggest further ways to help anyone feeling suicidal in custody.

5. Could the drug problem in prisons be eliminated if closed visits applied to everybody?

6. 'The most dramatic change in prisons has been Mandatory Drug Testing.' Discuss.

CHAPTER 4

Incentives and Release on Licence

THE INCENTIVE AND EARNED PRIVILEGE SYSTEM

In 1995 a National Framework for Incentives and Earned Privileges was devised and introduced into every prison during 1996. The main requirement for each establishment is to state clearly and publicly how the system operates and ensure everybody has access to this information.

The aims of the scheme are as follows:

- to have in place a system of privileges which are earned as a direct result of good performance and behaviour but which can be withdrawn if inmates fail to maintain an acceptable level of behaviour;
- to recognise and reward responsible behaviour;
- to encourage inmates to work and use their time constructively;
- to help sentenced inmates to progress through the prison system;
- to encourage inmates to conform;
- to develop a better disciplined, more controlled and safer environment for staff and inmates.

The basic requirement of all these schemes is to encourage co-operation. This can be achieved if everyone believes the scheme promotes justice and is administered fairly. Having an investment in the way things are run can act as an incentive to work hard and act maturely, provided a prisoner's efforts are recognised and rewarded appropriately.

In 1998 the system was reviewed and changes were introduced which restricted the level of private cash that inmates could accumulate in their spending account. The limit set is ten times the weekly limit that applies to the level of the incentive scheme they are on.

In order to cater for special need groups, private cash restrictions do not apply to those who meet the following criteria:

- women in mother-and-baby units can spend unlimited amounts of private cash on their babies, or on pregnancy related items;
- overseas phone calls are exempt for anyone with close relatives abroad or who normally lives abroad;

- anyone involved in legal proceedings who has exceptional costs;
- an unconvicted inmate who is continuing to keep his business running;
- inmates with exceptional circumstances.

Examining the pitfalls

The underlying assumption is that every privilege above the basic level has to be earned. There are three levels of privilege: basic, standard and enhanced. These are separate from the minimum standards that apply to inmates who are in the segregation unit undergoing punishment.

The statement in each establishment should set out the following:

- what privileges can be earned;
- details of the privileges that apply at each level and the criteria that need to be satisfied to earn and retain them;
- how privileges can be lost;
- details of the procedures that will be followed;
- the method of communicating the outcome of reviews, including how to lodge an appeal.

THE BASIC REGIME

Convicted inmates placed on the Basic regime are restricted to the following privileges:

1. *Private cash* – the allowance will be £2.50 per week.
2. *Visits* – two half-hour visits every 28 days, which take place in the normal visits area.
3. *Association* – this is the amount of time permitted to be spent out of a cell taking part in activities or mixing with other inmates. It is normally provided at a minimal level.

Inmates on the basic regime do not qualify for community visits, the enhanced earnings scheme, and cannot wear their own clothing.

An unconvicted prisoner on the basic regime is restricted to the following privileges:

1. *Private cash* – £15 per week. This limit is set at a higher level than for convicted inmates because they are not obliged to work.
2. *Visits* – a total of 1½ hours per week taken in the visits area.
3. *Association* – this should be provided at the level agreed within the establishment, normally a fairly minimal level.
4. *Wearing of own clothes* – this is an entitlement.

Inmates cannot be considered for community visits and any enhanced earnings scheme operating in the establishment.

Inmates wishing to avoid the basic regime should pay particular attention to the overall pattern of their institutional behaviour. The following issues need to receive particular attention:

- How well do they conform to the routines and rules?
- Are they regularly appearing on Governor's adjudications?
- Do they get on with other prisoners?
- How far do they co-operate with staff?
- Do they attend educational classes or a training course?
- Is their performance at work satisfactory?

Co-operating with, and becoming involved in, the Sentence Planning process shown is generally interpreted by staff as a willingness to use the custodial experience constructively. Similarly, forming a good relationship with the nominated personal officer is viewed positively.

Their attitude towards outside contacts is monitored including the level, frequency and nature of contacts with their family. Also important is any contact with the victim and contact with the outside Probation Service or other organisations.

The following may be included in local criteria to determine movement between the different levels of regime:

- *Non-violence* – an absence of violent threatening behaviour, bullying, offensive and aggressive language.
- *Non-discrimination* – an absence of racist, sexist and bigoted behaviour.
- *Civility* – considerate polite behaviour.
- *Mutual respect* – co-operation with the staff, compliance with lawful requests and an absence of devious or manipulative behaviour.
- *Treatment of others* – the nature of relationships with other inmates and whether they are exploitive or supportive.
- *Compliance of rules* – to what extent care is taken of prison property and equipment, how far they bend or break the regulations and take part in illicit activities like drug taking, hooch, gambling or the bullying of other inmates.
- *Personal hygiene* – to what extent they keep themselves and their cell clean and tidy.
- *Health and safety issues* – whether they are felt to pose a health hazard to others by the reckless way they use equipment, or whether they adhere to fire precautions and conform to smoking restrictions.
- *Achievements* – the amount of effort they put into their work or training course, offending behaviour group or educational classes. Recognition is given for achievements in terms of productivity and qualifications gained.

Inmates offering a reasonable level of co-operation are unlikely to be placed on the basic regime.

THE STANDARD REGIME

Once staff are satisfied that an inmate is unlikely to be problematic and they have completed the induction phase satisfactorily, they will be placed on the Standard regime. The recommended level of 'key earnable privileges' are laid down in the national framework. Those that apply to convicted prisoners are as follows:

1. *Private cash* – the allowance is £10 per week.
2. *Visits* – at least three visits every 28 days normally held in the visits area.
3. *Association* – this will correspond to whatever is normal in the establishment but will be set at a higher level than for those on the basic regime.
4. *Community visits* – anyone allocated to a resettlement prison or wing is allowed a weekly community visit. Those inmates in an open prison, suitable young offender or adult female prisoners are eligible for a monthly visit.
5. *Enhanced earnings scheme* – although standard regime inmates are eligible to be considered, priority will be given to those on the enhanced regime.
6. *Wearing of own clothes* – this is discretionary but in practice uncommon. However, women are able to wear their own clothes provided they are considered suitable.

An unconvicted prisoner on the standard regime can receive the following privileges:

1. *Private cash* – the allowance is £30 per week.
2. *Visits* – this will depend on the particular establishment but are set at a level higher than the basic regime and take place normally in the visits area.
3. *Association* – this is set at a higher level than for those on the basic regime.
4. *Wearing of own clothes* – this is an entitlement.
5. *Earned community visits* – this is not applicable.
6. *Enhanced earnings scheme* – priority is given to those on the enhanced regime.

THE ENHANCED REGIME

Governors have wide discretion to include a range of other additional privileges in their Incentive and Earned Privilege Schemes. This can include any or all of the following:

- allocating the best jobs to those on the enhanced regime, for example red-bands, kitchen party;
- additional items of cell furniture above the laid-down minimum standard;
- the use of cooking facilities on the wing;
- dining in association;
- electronic games;
- additional sessions in the gymnasium;
- access to laundry facilities;
- additional opportunities to use the library facilities;
- purchasing items by mail order;
- flexibility regarding mealtimes within defined time-bands;
- extra newspapers;
- having their own duvets as an alternative to prison bedding;
- any other items in possession that are permitted under the regulations, for instance, having their own curtains, a bedspread, flask, rug, or rechargeable batteries in a cell.

In October 1998 a pilot scheme on in-cell television was extended to all inmates, and became an earned but forfeitable privilege linked to local incentive and earned privilege schemes. However, all inmates on the basic regime are excluded from having this privilege, with priority being given to inmates on the enhanced regime. The sets, which receive the five main channels only, are provided by the Prison Service and are available to those who are eligible for a weekly rental of £1 per set. Currently this privilege is not widely available due to limited availability of in-cell electricity. However, about 10 per cent of the population should have access to this privilege during 1999.

The Governor is free to exercise his discretion about items to include provided they do not pose a security risk or contravene the volumetric control policy. This requires the total amount of personal possessions to be capable of fitting into two prison-issued boxes of a prescribed size.

There are strong incentives for inmates to conform and progress to the enhanced regime. The following privileges are laid down in the national framework as the recommended level for convicted prisoners on the enhanced regime:

1. *Private cash* – the allowance is £15 per week.
2. *Visits* – the level set is higher than for those on the standard regime. Where possible four or five one-hour visits should be allowed every 28 days. Flexibility exists over where these visits can take place and the type of conditions that apply.
3. *Association* – this is at a level higher than for the standard regime and can be up to 12 hours daily.
4. *Community visits* – for those in a resettlement prison or wing they are permitted one every week. Inmates in open conditions are normally allowed two visits each month. Other Category D inmates, selected Young Offenders and female prisoners are able to qualify for one on a monthly basis.
5. *Enhanced earnings scheme* – they are eligible for this privilege.
6. *Wearing of own clothes* – they are eligible for this concession.

Unconvicted inmates on the enhanced regime can receive the following privileges:

1. *Private cash* – the allowance is £30 per week.
2. *Visits* – while this depends on the level of resources available it is set at a level higher than applies on the standard regime. In practice, scope is limited given the limited facilities and level of overcrowding that is normal in a 'local' prison.
3. *Association* – this is set at a level higher than on the standard regime.
4. *Wearing of own clothes* – this is an entitlement.
5. *Community visits* – this does not apply to unconvicted inmates.
6. *Enhanced earnings scheme* – while theoretically eligible, in practice this is unlikely.

COMMUNITY VISITS

In 1996 Community Visits became an earnable privilege under the Incentive and Earned Privilege System. The Prison and Young Offender Institution Rules 6 (3) were altered in order to allow inmates to qualify for temporary release as a privilege under

Prison Rule 4 and YOI Rule 7. This means that those who meet the following criteria are eligible to be considered provided:

- at least a quarter of the sentence has been completed;
- they are on the standard or enhanced regime;
- they are located in a low security prison.

The objective is to reward those who behave responsibly and work well by allowing them to accompany their family or approved visitors, outside the prison. Before qualifying for community visits, inmates undergo a comprehensive risk assessment.

The following prisoners are eligible to be considered:

- Category D inmates;
- adult female prisoners and young offenders who have been assessed as suitable for outside activities;
- life sentence prisoners who have progressed to open conditions, subject to approval by Prison Service Headquarters.

Community visits normally take place at weekends and can last up to six hours. They can also be taken during the week if the Governor is satisfied that an individual's domestic circumstances justify exercising discretion in this way. Extended community visits can occur if they form part of the establishment's local incentive scheme for prisoners on the enhanced regime or if due to the location of the prison it is impractical to return to the prison within six hours. However, no one is permitted to be absent from the prison overnight.

A community visit may take place with a relative, probation officer, social worker or suitable responsible adult. Care will be taken to ensure that nobody takes part in any activity which might attract bad publicity, as this can jeopardise the chances of others from taking part in the scheme in the future.

Every inmate is issued with a licence which includes a number of conditions. A failure to comply can mean disciplinary action on his return to the establishment.

RISK ASSESSMENTS

Before an individual can be given any form of temporary release a comprehensive risk assessment must be carried out. Releasing anyone on a temporary licence carries with it the risk of re-offending so it is necessary to reduce those risks to an absolute minimum. A balance has to be struck between protecting the public interest and meeting the needs of individuals in prison custody. Sensible precautions are taken to weed out any applications where there are reasonable grounds to believe the terms of the licence may be broken.

The Governor takes the following factors into consideration when carrying out a risk assessment:

- any possible risk to the public;
- the likelihood that an offence will be committed while on temporary release;

- the risk of absconding;
- the possibility of a failure to abide by all the conditions on the licence and the likely consequences of such a failure.

When considering granting a temporary licence which involves an overnight stay the Governor considers the following additional factors:

- the availability of suitable accommodation;
- the acceptability of the reasons for approving release on licence.

Close attention is paid to the following factors:

- an individual's criminal record is carefully examined, particularly if there is a history of violence, sexual offences or arson. Particular care is taken with a Schedule 1 Offender, that is someone with convictions for violence against children and young people under the age of 18;
- their home circumstances and the ability of the inmate to cope with any problems that can be foreseen;
- the reaction of the victim;
- how well they have coped with previous periods of temporary release under licence;
- their overall behaviour and response in prison.

All inmates are subject to a Mandatory Drug Test which is carried out prior to anyone leaving for a period of temporary release. In the event of it proving positive the likelihood is the period of leave will be cancelled.

RELEASE ON TEMPORARY LICENCE

There are three types of release on temporary licence which cover the full range of circumstances that can arise. Anyone meeting the relevant criteria, and subject to a comprehensive risk assessment, can be considered to be allowed outside the establishment on licence:

1. *Compassionate licence*
   This is designed to cater for exceptional personal circumstances, for instance, attending the funeral of a close relative, a visit to a dying relative, where they are the primary carer for a child under 16 or elderly infirm close relative, in order to get married, attend a religious ceremony or attend a medical appointment.

2. *Facility licence*
   This allows the opportunity to take part in a Community Service project, attend an educational or life skills course, undertake relevant employment training and other activities which include an element of reparation to the community. Alternatively it can be used where there is a need to act as a police witness, to visit a legal adviser in

person or to attend civil proceedings, such as an application for custody or adoption. For young offenders serving under 12 months, it can be used to attend job interviews, obtain accommodation or prevent the possible loss of existing accommodation.

3. *Resettlement licence*
   The aim of this form of temporary release is to support and assist inmates to maintain family ties. This can include making arrangements to obtain suitable employment, training on release or to enable them to obtain suitable accommodation for occupation on release.

Anyone falling into any of the following categories is not eligible to apply:

- Category A prisoners;
- on the escape list (an E list prisoner);
- unconvicted;
- convicted but unsentenced;
- subject to extradition proceedings or a deportee;
- a sentenced prisoner remanded or awaiting sentence for further offences;
- Category B prisoners are not eligible for facility licences;
- a life sentence prisoner, unless they are in Category C conditions with a provisional release date or within one year of their review by the Parole Board.

An inmate in one of the following groups will receive special attention:

- a life sentence prisoner;
- if a parole or supervision licence has been revoked;
- a prisoner diagnosed as suffering with a mental health problem;
- a civil prisoner;
- a fine defaulter;
- an appellant;
- anyone detained by the immigration authorities under the Immigration Act 1971 and anyone who is a United States serviceman.

COMPASSIONATE LICENCE

There are no specific criteria laid down for a compassionate licence unless an inmate falls within one of the ineligible categories or is serving a life sentence and has not had a full risk assessment completed (see Figure 4.1). A lifer without a provisional release date can be considered after he has spent six months in open conditions. A lifer who has received a provisional release date becomes eligible four months after receiving it.

Release on a compassionate licence can be granted on an accompanied release basis where it is considered desirable.

Attendance at funerals of close relatives or visits to a dying relative are normally allowed irrespective of the prisoner's security category, but may mean being escorted and handcuffed at all times, and in the case of Category A prisoners subject to elaborate and intensive security precautions.

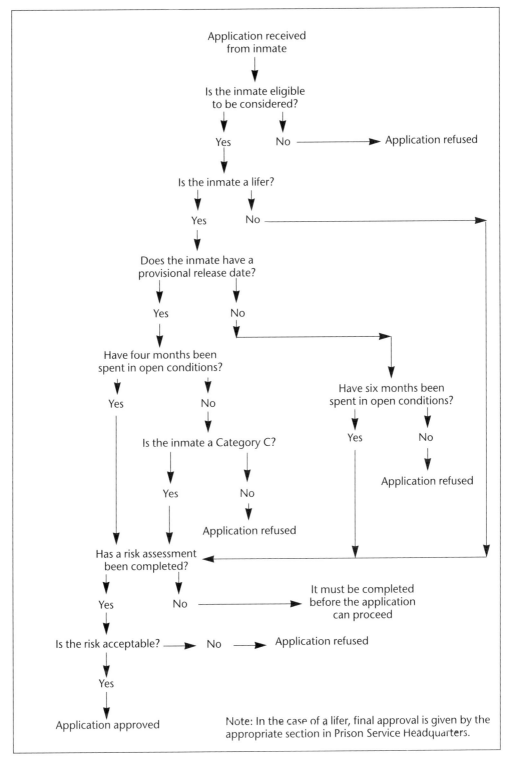

Figure 4.1: Compassionate release flowchart (all inmates)

A compassionate licence is normally limited to a minimal period outside the establishment, sometimes a matter of a few hours. However, it can be extended for to up to five days in a month if necessary. For instance, in the case of having to attend as an in-patient for hospital treatment this limit can be waived.

Compassionate licences are appropriate in the following circumstances:

- visits to terminally ill close relatives including those *in loco parentis*;
- attending the funeral of a close relative;
- other tragic personal or family circumstances;
- in the case of a primary carer, that is someone with sole responsibility for caring for a youngster or a seriously disabled close relative, in order to visit them. For instance, a female prisoner with a toddler in a mother-and-baby unit who needed to receive outside medical treatment or to undergo an operation;
- to get married in the community;
- attending medical appointments at an outside clinic, hospital or to undergo surgery;
- young offenders may visit their parents, or anyone *in loco parentis* who is unable to visit due to illness or incapacity;
- any inmate held in open conditions or in a resettlement prison may attend the main weekly service of religious worship outside the establishment.

FACILITY LICENCE

Once a quarter of the sentence has been served, including any time spent on remand, inmates become eligible to be considered for release under a facility licence (see Figure 4.2). It is necessary to demonstrate that granting a facility licence will help the rehabilitative process and assist them to lead useful and law-abiding lives after release. Someone serving a life sentence in open conditions will normally qualify once they have completed eight weeks in the establishment. Alternatively, they can qualify if they are being held in Category C conditions and have either received a provisional release date or are within one year of their Parole Board review. Facility licences must not be used for any social or recreational activities or for any purpose that will attract reasonable public concern. Normally a facility licence is only issued when it cannot be more appropriately deferred to later in the sentence, or the reason for the application dealt with under the criteria applicable to approving a resettlement licence.

A facility licence is normally approved for daytime activities of up to five consecutive days' duration. This usually includes the following:

- approved educational programmes;
- outdoor activities such as Outward Bound courses;
- Employment Training workshops and community projects;
- working out schemes involving paid work in the community;
- Pre-release Employment Schemes (PRES) designed for those in the final months of a lengthy sentence;
- an unescorted transfer in the case where someone has been downgraded from Category C to D. This does not however apply to lifers;

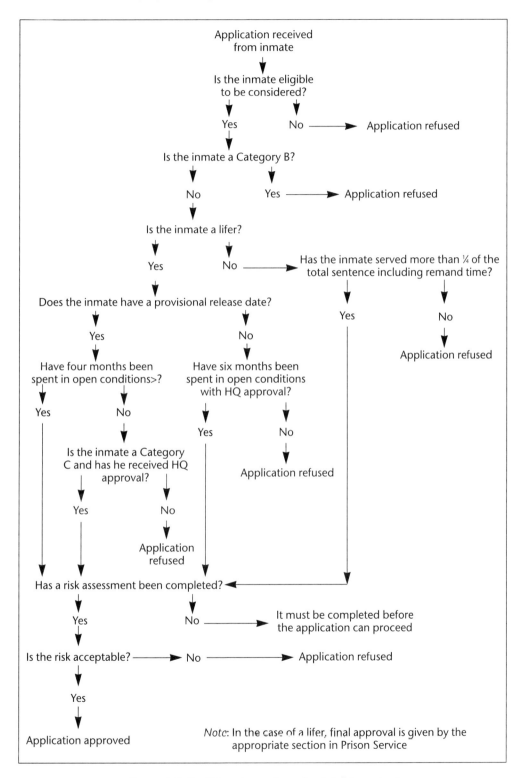

Figure 4.2: Facility release flowchart (all inmates)

- participating at a legal case conference where their presence is required;
- attending a court hearing where required as a witness in a criminal case, or attending an inquest in a Coroner's Court.

Young offenders can be considered for release on a facility licence to:

- attend job and accommodation interviews, providing they are serving under 12 months;
- resolve serious housing and accommodation problems;
- take part in adventure training schemes including Outward Bound activities and the Duke of Edinburgh Award Scheme;
- take part in team sports, particularly when they represent the establishment, and can build links locally.

Young offenders and inmates aged 18–24 serving less than 12 months can be released to attend job interviews under the Government's 'Welfare to Work' scheme.

RESETTLEMENT LICENCE

The Resettlement Licence Eligibility Date depends on a number of factors; but provided an inmate does not fall into any of the ineligible groups and has completed a risk assessment satisfactorily, it is likely he will be given consideration (see Figures 4.3 and 4.4).

The criteria for those sentenced to a fixed sentence after 1 October 1992, when the Criminal Justice Act 1991 came into effect, are as follows:

1. A young offender sentenced to less than 12 months custody is eligible three months after his date of sentence, or four weeks before the Automatic Release Date (ARD), whichever is the sooner. Adults however are not eligible unless they are serving over 12 months.
2. An adult or young offender sentenced from between 12 months to under four years is eligible after serving one-third of his sentence or four months after his date of sentence, whichever is the later date.
3. An adult or young offender serving over four years becomes eligible once half of his sentence has been completed which coincides with the Parole Eligibility Date (PED). If he receives a favourable decision about parole by the PED he can normally go on resettlement leave within four weeks of his release date.
4. If parole is refused an inmate must wait six months from the PED date, or the date of the refusal letter, whichever is sooner, before he can be released on resettlement licence. The period of ineligibility is three months for young offenders.
5. If parole is subsequently refused he must wait a further two months from the date on the refusal letter before qualifying for a resettlement licence.
6. A lifer who has received a provisional release date becomes eligible four months from the date he was advised. Otherwise he may have to be in open conditions for nine months before he can be considered.

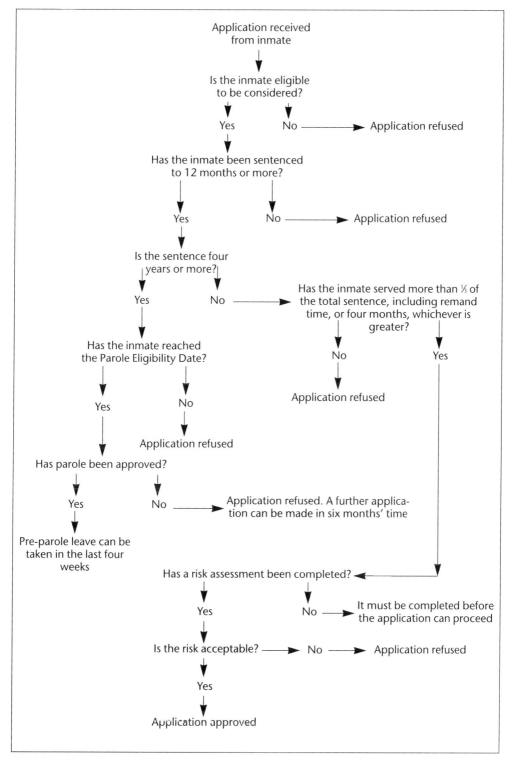

Figure 4.3: Resettlement release flowchart (for a determinate sentence)

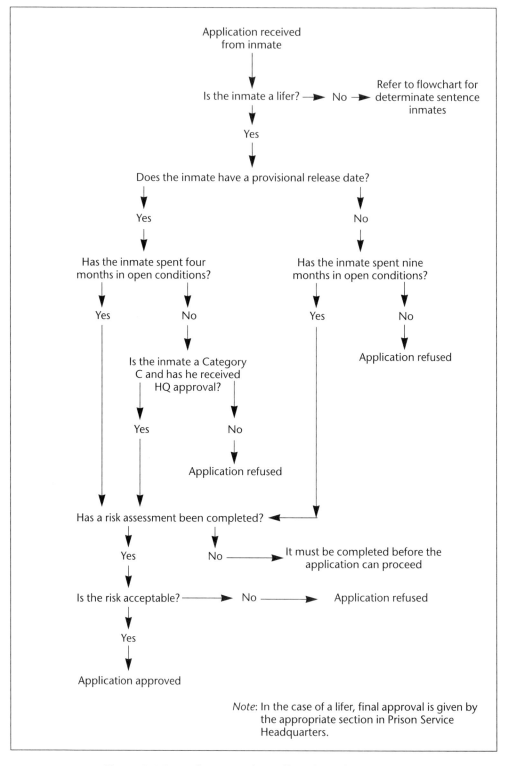

Figure 4.4: Resettlement release flowchart (lifers only)

A resettlement licence normally lasts from between one and five days. Periods of resettlement leave can be taken as frequently as every eight weeks provided they correspond with the individual's needs as identified in the Sentence Plan. Resettlement leave can be taken at weekends except for a life sentence prisoner who is restricted to weekdays initially. Resettlement leave can be used for the following purposes:

- interviews with prospective employers;
- visits to aftercare hostels;
- home visits to develop family ties;
- attending workshops organised by the Probation Service aimed at addressing specific problems applicable to the individual;
- Community service placements arranged by the national Community Service Volunteers (CSV);
- participating in working-out schemes. This is only applicable if they are already at a resettlement prison or attending a pre-release employment scheme hostel.

ACCOMPANIED RELEASE ON TEMPORARY LICENCE

Despite carrying out a risk assessment and deciding an inmate is suitable to be released on licence, it may be considered appropriate, as well as supportive, to make it a condition of the licence that the inmate is accompanied by a member of staff.

Individual circumstances will vary considerably, but it may be a viable option where it is felt the presence of an officer, or member of staff, could contribute to the success of a visit outside the establishment. Examples of when this might be appropriate would include accompanying an inmate to the funeral of a close relative or attending an interview with them at a hostel where they hope to live on discharge. Anyone who has been in prison for a long time may find being accompanied by someone they trust particularly supportive.

ESCORTED ABSENCES

If an inmate is not eligible, or is considered unsuitable for any form of release on temporary licence, the Governor can exercise his discretion under Prison Rules to approve an escorted absence. It may be very important to attend the funeral of a close relative but inappropriate on security grounds for them to be allowed out of the custody and control of prison staff.

BREACHES OF TRUST

Despite all the precautions that are taken to minimise risks, things can still go wrong. Each establishment has in place a series of checks aimed at reducing the likelihood of a breach of the temporary licence conditions from occurring, which include the following:

1. Prior to going on temporary release, inmates are subject to a drug test. If it proves positive this will invariably lead to the cancellation of the privilege and result in a disciplinary charge.

2. Spot checks are carried out to ensure that individuals arrive at a hostel or job interview. These checks can involve staff visiting local public houses to check unauthorised visits have not been made while outside the prison on licence.

3. A failure to return back to the prison on time will normally lead to disciplinary action unless the circumstances are exceptional and the inmate's version of events can be corroborated. It also seriously jeopardises the possibility of any further periods of temporary release being approved in the future if trust has been abused.

4. If a criminal offence is committed or an inmate fails to return to the prison on time, contrary to the Prisoners (Return to Custody) Act 1995, this is viewed very seriously by both the police and prison authorities. If eligible for parole such a breach of trust is brought to the attention of the Parole Board. In the case of a lifer it may result in a provisional release date being revised.

5. Any reported misbehaviour or any incident that occurs which leads to an arrest, irrespective of whether proceedings result, is likely to lead to recall from release on temporary licence. If this happens the inmate will be arrested and taken to the nearest police station to await collection by prison staff.

MAKING AN APPLICATION FOR TEMPORARY RELEASE

The procedure for applying for any form of temporary release is as follows:

1. An application form is completed and handed to the wing manager.

2. Applications for resettlement leave are considered by a Board which considers a home circumstances report from the outside probation officer, a risk assessment completed by prison staff, and other reports from staff who work in the prison and are able to comment on the attitude, general behaviour and response of the inmate while in custody, as well as level of trustworthiness.

3. The Board membership includes, as a minimum, the governor grade with overall responsibility for residential units, the personal officer and the prison-based probation officer. In the case of a life sentence prisoner other staff are invited to the Board.

4. The Board invites the inmate to attend and add anything to their statement of application. They are likely to be asked several questions about their circumstances, before the Panel members retire to consider whether to recommend the Governor approves the application.

5. The Board may decide to contact outside agencies before finalising its assessment of the degree of risk a case presents. This can include consultations with the police, the probation service and where serious sexual or violent offences have been committed, with the victim and their family.

Understanding the process

All requests for temporary release have to be approved by the Governor. Where inmates are located in a prison run by a private company the Controller appointed by the Home Secretary makes the decision to authorise temporary release. In both instances the process followed is the same.

Inmates are expected to save a certain amount of money from their earnings or private cash prior to going on resettlement licence. The reason for this is to ensure they have sufficient pocket money to meet personal needs while away from the prison and are not tempted to commit crime. The amount required to be saved varies between establishments and is at the Governor's discretion.

They are normally given a travel warrant or the cost of fares for the return journey home, together with a modest subsistence allowance. In the event of unforeseen expenses arising while absent from the prison, for instance losing the return ticket, contact must be made with the community-based supervising probation officer. Anybody losing a railway or bus ticket is likely to be required to reimburse the prison authorities. Losing a ticket is not an acceptable reason for returning late. Too many prisoners have used that excuse in the past for prison staff to be other than sceptical.

An inmate who becomes ill while on resettlement licence and whose return is going to be delayed must immediately contact both the supervising officer named on the licence and the penal establishment. The inmate's general practitioner or a hospital doctor has to verify in writing that he is so physically incapacitated as to be unfit to travel back or make his way to the nearest penal establishment. Prison staff are careful to investigate the circumstances and if feasible make arrangements for an individual to be accommodated locally in custody. In the past some prisoners have tried this ruse to gain an extension of resettlement leave with their families.

Finally, anyone who feels aggrieved at a decision not to grant temporary leave can ask for the decision to be put in writing, then lodge an appeal through the formal Request and Complaints system.

HOME DETENTION CURFEW

The Crime and Disorder Act 1998 allows for inmates serving short sentences to be considered for release on licence two months before their Automatic Release Date on Home Detention Curfew. The scheme, introduced on 28 January 1999, does not apply to juveniles or young offenders under the age of 18. Any inmate required to register under Part One of the Sex Offenders Act 1997, or liable to deportation under the Immigration Act 1971, or subject to a Hospital Order, or who has been returned to custody for a breach of licence or who has committed an offence before the *at risk* period of a sentence has expired, is ineligible. Violent and sex offenders serving an extended sentence which involves supervision under Section 58 of the Crime and Disorder Act 1998 cannot be considered.

Inmates serving short sentences of between three and four months are eligible for release on *home detention curfew* after they have served one month in custody. Those serving sentences of between four and eight months are eligible for consideration after they have served one-quarter of their sentence (including time spent on remand).

Those inmates serving sentences of three months or over and under four years, are eligible to be released on licence up to two months before their Automatic Release Date.

All inmates eligible for consideration under the scheme are given an information leaflet on reception titled 'Home Detention Curfew: Information for Prisoners' and are subject to two risk assessments procedures. The *standard assessment* applies to all inmates and considers existing reports from the police and home probation service. The *enhanced assessment* involves a more detailed risk assessment of those inmates serving sentences of more than 12 months who do not have a successful record of temporary release; or who are scored as a 'high risk' on the risk predictor factors for violent or sex offences; or are considered under the standard assessment to require closer scrutiny.

Unless an inmate would spend less than 14 days on a home detention curfew licence, or is ineligible for the scheme, no inmate will be refused release on home detention curfew until an enhanced assessment has first taken place.

The enhanced assessment is completed by the *Home Detention Board* which comprises a governor grade, a seconded probation officer and the inmate's personal officer. The recommendations of the Home Detention Board are considered by the Governor who makes the final decision. An inmate refused home detention curfew is informed of the reason for that decision. The grounds for refusal are normally as follows:

- an unacceptable risk to the victim or members of the public;
- a pattern of offending which indicates an unacceptable risk of offending during the home curfew period;
- a high risk of failing to comply with the conditions of home detention curfew;
- a lack of a suitable address.

Inmates refused home detention curfew may appeal against the decision using the normal Request and Complaint system. Those inmates approved for home detention curfew are subject to standard conditions for the curfew hours, which will be for a minimum of nine hours a day at a suitable approved address.

Any inmate who violates the curfew or damages the equipment is liable to recall to custody by the Adult Males Parole and Lifer Group (AMPLG) in Prison Service Headquarters, who decide whether or not to revoke the licence.

CASE STUDIES

Rudd Basho absconds from resettlement leave

Rudd Basho has served four months of his sentence and applies for resettlement leave to be taken in the month prior to his Automatic Release Date. His plan is to stay with his parents and seek accommodation in advance of his release, in order to set up home with his girlfriend Lola who is expecting their first baby. His request for resettlement leave is approved and he stays with his parents and reports to his probation officer as required under the terms of his licence. During his resettlement leave Lola goes into labour early and gives birth to the baby who unfortunately experiences serious and worrying feeding difficulties. Lola becomes very depressed and Rudd finds he is unable to cope with leaving Lola to manage alone. He decides not to return to the establishment but within 48 hours he is arrested and returned to the establishment where he is charged with a disciplinary offence. The Governor accepts there are mitigating circumstances but as he has abused the trust placed in him, he delays his conditional release date by 28 days as a punishment.

Peter Miles applies to attend his father's funeral

Peter Miles is serving five years and has completed 15 months of his sentence. He has progressed to the enhanced regime and staff consider him to be a model prisoner. Peter's father dies suddenly and he applies for compassionate leave in order to attend the funeral. A risk assessment is carried out but although his response during his current custodial sentence is excellent, his record of previous offending coupled with the seriousness of his current drug-related offence leads the Governor to conclude the risks are finely balanced as it is still early in his sentence. However, he approves a compassionate licence, with the proviso that he is accompanied by his personal officer.

Paddy Naughtie goes on a community service placement

Paddy Naughtie is a lifer who has recently been transferred to open conditions and has been told that his provisional release date is in twelve months' time. He applies to take part in the Community Service programme and contribute to a project that involves redecorating a church hall. A comprehensive risk assessment is completed and Paddy is released on a weekday facility licence. While on the project a member of staff pays occasional visits to check he is working satisfactorily and complying with the conditions of his licence. Paddy demonstrates his trustworthiness and after nine months in open conditions he is granted resettlement leave to stay with his girlfriend's family, where he plans to live on release.

Nicola Harrington is placed on the basic regime

Nicola Harrington has an attitude problem. She feels aggrieved that the courts did not take pity on her plight, as she is a battered partner who is six months pregnant and is feeling very anti-authority. Her behaviour is problematic, she is abusive to staff, disobeys orders and is generally unco-operative including failing to maintain reasonable standards of hygiene in her cell. Nicola is warned several times about her poor attitude but she fails to take any notice. After she has been on the wing for a month her progress is reviewed at the Incentive and Earned Privilege Board. Wing staff and the probation officer attend, and a report is received from the the Kitchen who employ her. The consensus is that she has failed to co-operate or modify her general response despite being given several opportunities to improve. Following the review board she is called up by the wing manager and advised she has been placed on the basic regime but that her progress will be reviewed in one month's time. The effect is that her allowance to spend private cash in the prison shop is reduced from £10 to £2.50 per week, her allowance to visits is reduced from three extended visits every 28 days to two half-hour visits every 28 days, and instead of having association with the other women on the wing every night she is restricted to three nights each week. Nicola is encouraged to improve her behaviour and assured she can progress back to the standard regime next month if she responds accordingly.

CHECKLIST

- When is it essential to carry out a comprehensive risk assessment?
- How do prisoners qualify for community visits?
- Which prisoners are ineligible for temporary release on compassionate licence?
- Define an *in loco parentis* relationship.
- Under what circumstances can a lifer be considered for a facility licence?
- What is the membership of the resettlement leave board for determinate sentence prisoners?
- What are a prisoner's responsibilities if admission to hospital for treatment becomes necessary while on resettlement leave?
- Under what circumstances can a prisoner be recalled from temporary release?
- When would accompanied release on temporary licence be appropriate?
- What is the avenue of appeal against a refusal to grant temporary release by the resettlement leave board?
- How often can a resettlement licence be approved?
- What is the relationship between the Incentive and Earned Privilege System and release on temporary licence?
- How might a breach of the conditions of temporary licences affect a lifer?
- Which prisoners qualify for release on Home Detention Curfew?
- What is the role of the Home Detention Board?

DISCUSSION POINTS

1. Examine the case for prisoner 'compacts' to be an integral part of the sentence planning process.

2. 'Placing prisoners on the basic regime is a form of disciplinary action and contradicts the principles of natural justice.' Discuss.

3. Consider ways in which a life sentence prisoner can be prepared for release on parole.

4. Examine how far it is possible to balance the risks to the public of releasing prisoners on temporary licence against the need to assist prisoners with their rehabilitation.

5. Describe the procedure for dealing with applications for resettlement leave. In what ways could the process be improved?

6. 'The interests of victims are ignored when prisoners are considered for temporary release.' Discuss.

CHAPTER 5

The Request and Complaint System

UNDERSTANDING THE SYSTEM

It is important that inmates clearly understand what is expected of them in prison and that they co-operate with staff. This avoids difficulties arising and enables them to concentrate on using their time in custody constructively.

Problems inevitably arise on occasions, so knowing how the system operates is invaluable (see Figure 5.1). There are three recognised ways to raise a request or complaint:

1. Informally at an establishment level; initially raised verbally, but if unresolved it can be put in writing and raised formally.
2. A formal appeal to Prison Service Headquarters.
3. Raising the complaint externally by seeking help from a legal adviser, an MP, petitioning Parliament, or by contacting a special interest group for assistance.

The first approach should be to discuss the problem with a wing landing officer, preferably the inmate's personal officer, who should be able to offer advice about how to proceed if unable to resolve the difficulty personally.

Making an application to see the wing manager is the next stage. A record of the application should be made in the wing application book together with the answer given. If an individual is still unhappy with the outcome he can make a Governor's Application. This means a senior manager of the prison or YOI sees him to discuss the matter. Although inmates do not have the right to see the Governor, normally they would see either a Principal Officer or a Governor grade with responsibility for casework matters on the wing.

The simplest and quickest way to resolve problems is by making a verbal application. However, anyone continuing to feel dissatisfied has little alternative other than to make a formal application.

AIRING GRIEVANCES

Following the prison disturbances that occurred in 1990, the Woolf Report recommended that greater emphasis should be placed on ensuring justice for all prisoners and that reasons should be given for any negative decisions.

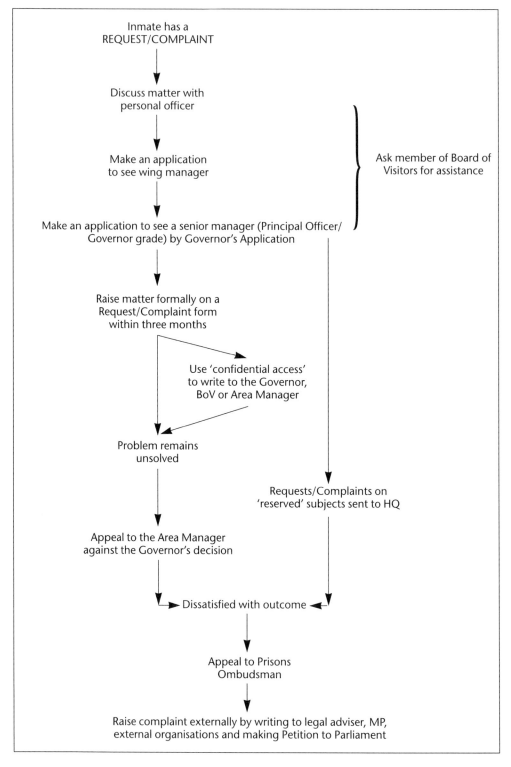

Figure 5.1: Request and complaint flowchart

These principles have been incorporated into the Request and Complaint system, which aims to encourage good relationships between staff and prisoners. This reduces tension and anxieties while encouraging inmates to appreciate they are not powerless and do not have to tolerate unfair treatment.

It is in everyone's interests that requests and complaints are looked into objectively and fairly. When occasions arise that a genuine grievance is identified, it should be promptly remedied.

The system includes a confidential appeal system which is external to the establishment and complies with European Prison Rule 42 (3).

The overall aim is to deal informally with requests and minor complaints. Most establishments have a personal officer scheme in operation; personal officers should take the lead in problem-solving, given that 95 per cent of applications are made to wing staff. In order to encourage this to happen, wing applications should be held in private on a daily basis at a predetermined time.

If the procedure for dealing with verbal applications informally fails to resolve the problem, then the individual should resort to the formal process of making a request or complaint.

MAKING A FORMAL APPLICATION

A formal application means asking for a *Request/Complaint Form* to be issued (see p. 164). This form is numbered and a record kept in the prison of when and to whom it has been issued. The form is self-explanatory and invites the complainant to state their request or complaint fully, indicating what action they would like taken in order to resolve the problem.

Since June 1997 a written request or complaint has to be made within three months of the problem arising and unless there are very good reasons, formal applications submitted outside the time limits will not be considered.

Once the form has been returned to the wing office it is considered by a senior manager and a written reply follows, normally within seven days. If the issue raised is complicated, an interim reply may be sent outlining what action the establishment is taking and when a final decision can be expected.

A complaint about property lost when the inmate transferred needs to be investigated by both establishments involved, which takes time. The interim reply would outline the nature of the enquiries that are being pursued and the likely timescale before a complete answer can be expected.

If it is established that the item of property was lost in transit then negotiations about an appropriate level of compensation may follow. This is often the case if no receipt or any supporting evidence is available to establish the value of the missing item.

THE REQUEST AND COMPLAINT SYSTEM

If an inmate makes a verbal application and follows it up with a formal written request but is still dissatisfied with the outcome, there are two other possibilities:

- make an application to see the Board of Visitors;
- appeal to the Area Manager.

If an inmate applies to see the Board of Visitors (BoV) he will normally be expected to have exhausted the internal complaints system although there is no restriction on anyone approaching a member of the BoV any time it is felt to be helpful. The BoV will consider all the available and relevant information including any formal replies that have been received from senior staff. The Board meets with the Governor on a monthly basis and may invite the Governor to reconsider a decision, raise the matter with the Area Manager as a Board or even write to the Home Secretary if they feel sufficiently strongly about the grievance that has been raised.

The other option is to appeal to the Area Manager. This means requesting a *Request/Complaint Appeal Form* (see p. 166) and setting out fully the grounds for the appeal. The Area Manager is a very senior manager based at Prison Service Headquarters in London, with operational responsibility for around 15 penal establishments.

Some matters can only be decided at a Headquarters level and these are called *reserved* subjects. They include the following:

- parole decisions;
- adjudication appeals;
- complaints about medical treatment;
- categorisation and allocation decisions;
- Category A status prisoner matters;
- lifer management status issues;
- appeals against deportation;
- any matter concerning conviction or the sentence imposed;
- complaints relating to refusal to admit to mother-and-baby units or any aspect of the care of women with babies;
- applications for artificial insemination by married couples;
- requests for early release;
- appeals against establishment decisions.

A *Request/Complaint Form* is issued in the normal way but once completed and handed in, it is forwarded directly to Headquarters. A reply normally arrives within six weeks although some complicated matters can take longer than this to investigate and resolve.

RAISING A SERIOUS COMPLAINT

A serious complaint can be raised confidentially by writing directly to the Governor, Area Manager or Chairman of the Board of Visitors. This is achieved by setting out the complaint and placing it in an envelope marked 'Prisoner's Confidential Access' before handing it in to the wing office. The letter will be passed to the addressee who may decide to deal with it through the normal channels and pass it to a senior manager to answer. If the complaint is a serious allegation against a member of staff, then the recipient can arrange for an investigation to be conducted.

Complaints against staff are always treated seriously and can lead to disciplinary action or dismissal under certain circumstances. If a member of staff has acted contrary to the rules and regulations the following facts should be clearly set out:

- a full description of what happened;
- details of when the incident occurred;
- the location of the incident;
- a full account of what happened and what was said;
- the names of any witnesses;
- other relevant information and any supporting corroborative evidence.

The Governor will ask an impartial senior member of staff to investigate the complaint. If he considers the allegations to be sufficently serious a senior manager from another establishment may be asked to lead the enquiry. He will interview the inmate, talk to the member of staff who is the subject of the complaint and interview any named witnesses.

Once the investigation has been concluded the Governor will write to the inmate advising of the findings and whether he intends to take any further action. The Governor has to decide whether:

(a) the complaint is justified;
(b) disciplinary action is appropriate;
(c) it appears a criminal offence has been committed and it is appropriate to refer the matter to the police to investigate with a view to taking proceedings.

The Request and Complaints system is designed to provide a fair and impartial investigation when something goes wrong. If the confidential access facility is misused, with inmates regularly making false and malicious complaints against staff, everybody's time is wasted and the system becomes devalued.

If an individual decides at any time to withdraw a written request or complaint or an appeal, this is simply achieved. A member of staff can retrieve the original form, the inmate writes 'Withdrawn' across it and signs and dates the statement.

THE BOARD OF VISITORS

Everyone has the legal right to speak to a member of the Board of Visitors (BoV) privately and discuss any complaint or problem with them.

The Board of Visitors have a responsibility, as part of their 'watchdog' role, to satisfy themselves that all those in custody are being looked after properly and treated fairly. This includes listening to applications and looking into any complaints inmates express about their treatment in prison.

Inmates are entitled to write to the Chairman of the Board of Visitors using confidential access, but it is for the Chairman to decide whether to personally follow up the complaint or to refer it for the Governor to deal with, or raise the matter directly with Prison Service Headquarters.

The Board of Visitors are members of the public appointed by the Secretary of State under section 6(2) of the Prison Act 1952 with clearly laid-down responsibilities for each establishment. Their responsibilities include the following:

- to listen to any requests or complaints that inmates wish to make, and to consult any prison records including relevant case files;
- to check regularly that the quality of food being provided is satisfactory;
- to make regular monthly visits to the establishment on a rota basis, attending at any time of the day or night;
- to follow up any concerns they become aware of concerning an individual's mental and physical health;
- to extend and authorise a period of segregation under Prison Rule 43(2) which the Governor judges is for the good order and discipline of the establishment, or is in the individual's own interests. This segregation can last for up to a month in the case of adults or 14 days for young offenders and can be extended provided it is regularly reviewed;
- to carry out enquiries on behalf of the Secretary of State and bring any serious concerns to his attention;
- to prepare an annual report for the Secretary of State which can be shared with the media.

Although the BoV have no executive powers, in the sense that they do not have the authority to directly intervene in the way the establishment is run, they can make representations to the Governor on an inmate's behalf if they have concerns about his treatment.

Before 1992 the BoV had authority to deal with serious disciplinary offences but this created confusion in some prisoners' minds about their independence. The *Woolf Report* recommended that the adjudicatory powers of the Board of Visitors were removed and this view was endorsed by the Home Secretary.

Members of the BoV are still selected by, and accountable to the Home Secretary. They come from a diverse range of backgrounds and include all ethnic origins, but tend to be respectable law-abiding members of the local community who have a genuine interest in public service and penal issues.

APPEALING TO THE PRISONS OMBUDSMAN

Since October 1995 there has existed a formal avenue of appeal against decisions taken at Prison Service Headquarters. The Prisons Ombudsman was appointed together with three Assistant Prisons Ombudsmen following a recommendation contained in the *Woolf Report* into 'Prison Disturbances April 1990' which was accepted by the Home Secretary.

The Prisons Ombudsman provides an independent and impartial avenue of appeal which can be pursued after the internal Request and Complaints process has been exhausted.

Most complaints about treatment in custody can be investigated by the Prisons Ombudsman, provided contact is made within one month of receiving a final reply from Prison Service Headquarters. If an appeal has been lodged and it is being dealt with by the Area Manager or Prisoner Casework Unit, and a reply has not been received within six weeks, inmates are free to complain directly to the Prisons Ombudsman. This is equally applicable to those who are accommodated in a contracted-out prison, who are entitled to write to him.

Some grievances do not come under his jurisdiction and they are as follows:

- decisions taken by other government bodies, for instance the police, the courts, the Parole Board and the Immigration Service;
- any matter where criminal proceedings or civil litigation is in progress;
- any clinical judgments made by the Prison Medical Officer;
- decisions taken by the Home Secretary which relate to the arrangements for reviewing or releasing a prisoner serving a life sentence.

Anyone wishing to complain to the Prisons Ombudsman can either write to him directly at public expense, or hand in a letter to the wing office marked 'Prisoner's Confidential Access' for forwarding by the establishment.

The address of the Prisons Ombudsman is as follows: Ashley House, 2 Monck Street, London SW1P 2BQ.

All replies are clearly marked 'Prisons Ombudsman' and must be handed to the addressee unopened.

Once the Prisons Ombudsman agrees to investigate a complaint he will be given a copy of the original complaint and any responses made by Prison Service officials. He has complete freedom to see copies of any Prison Service documents and can contact any member of staff or prisoner, in any way he chooses. If necessary, he can make arrangements to interview relevant personnel including the complainant.

There are some understandable constraints on him; for instance, he cannot examine an individual's medical record without his permission. Neither can he divulge to an inmate or any member of the public any confidential material which is classified information or which might prejudice the security of the prison, be contrary to the interests of national security and which could put the safety of any person at risk.

The Prisons Ombudsman deals promptly with all complaints and after investigating a matter, will formally respond within eight weeks. His findings and recommendations are always copied to Prison Service Headquarters where the Director General of the Prison Service is obliged to consider his conclusions and respond within six weeks stating what action he intends to take.

The Prison Service is keen to co-operate with any investigations initiated by the Prisons Ombudsman and is predisposed to act on any recommendations he makes.

Each year the Prisons Ombudsman publishes an Annual Report which includes a section outlining the response from the Prison Service to his recommendations.

KNOWING EXTERNAL AVENUES OF REDRESS

Anyone who writes to an outside individual or organisation with a request or complaint should first use the internal complaints procedure. Otherwise if an outsider takes up the matter with the Home Office or Prison Service Headquarters, the complaint will be passed to the establishment to answer. This simply means that any grievance takes longer to be considered than if it had been raised with the Prison Governor initially.

On the other hand, if the internal avenues of complaint have been exhausted such a complaint is given priority and dealt with without delay.

Some of the options available are as follows:

- *Writing to their Member of Parliament at the House of Commons*
  Staff can advise which MP represents a particular constituency, or alternatively they can consult the Prison Library. Inmates should include their home address on any correspondence they send to an MP as a constituent.
- *Contacting a legal adviser*
- *Sending a petition to the Queen*
  Everyone has a constitutional right to petition the Queen. This is achieved by simply writing a petition in the form of a letter to the Queen and sending it either to Prison Service Headquarters or directly to Her Majesty, Buckingham Palace, London.
- *Sending a petition to Parliament*
  The right to petition Parliament about a grievance is a fundamental constitutional principle. Inmates can petition Parliament provided they address the petition to a named Member of Parliament, which is normally their own constituency MP. Similarly, a petition can be sent to the House of Lords by writing to a named member. A petition to the House of Commons must be written out by hand and worded as follows:
  > *To the Honourable the Commons of the United Kingdom of Great Britain and Northern Ireland in Parliament assembled*
  > *The Humble petition of* (inserting their full name)
  > *Sheweth That* (at this point the inmate should outline his request or complaint)
  > *Wherefore your Petitioner prays that your honourable House* (at this point the inmate should state what he wants done about his grievance)
  > *And your Petitioner as in duty bound, will ever pray* (this is how the petition is concluded and is followed by the inmate's signature and address).

- *Sending a petition to a Member of the European Parliament*
  Inmates can petition their Member of the European Parliament in the same way as
  they write to their MP.
- *Sending a petition to the European Commission of Human Rights*
  The European Court of Human Rights can be petitioned provided inmates wait no
  longer than six months after exhausting all the domestic avenues of complaint
  before making their appeal. The address to write to is: Secretary General, Council
  of Europe, 67006 Strasbourg, France.
- *Writing to the Parliamentary Commissioner for Administration*
  The Parliamentary Commissioner for Administration is the same as the Parliamen-
  tary Ombudsman. He can only investigate a complaint if asked to do so by an MP
  so anyone wishing to have their case investigated should ask their MP to make the
  referral.
- *Complaining to the Chief Officer of Police*
  Writing to the Chief Officer of Police is appropriate if there is sufficient evidence to
  support an allegation that a criminal offence has been committed.
- *Submitting a claim to the Criminal Injuries Compensation Board*
  The Criminal Injuries Compensation Board examines claims for compensation if
  the victim of a violent crime makes an application. The address is: Criminal
  Injuries Compensation Board, Tay House, 300 Bath Street, Glasgow G2 4JR.

  The Criminal Injuries Compensation Board will send an application form for
  completion, which asks for an outline of the injuries and the circumstances in
  which the injuries were sustained, what treatment was given and to whom the
  incident was reported. It will thoroughly investigate all claims and may require the
  victim to attend a full hearing.
- *Complaining to the Commission for Racial Equality*
  The Commission for Racial Equality investigates allegations of racial discrimination which are contrary to the Race Relations Act 1976. The address is:
  Commission for Racial Equality, Elliot House, 10–12 Allington Street, London
  SW1E 5EH.

There are many organisations willing to assist prisoners with advice and guidance.
However, they have no formal powers of intervention under the Request/Complaints
system. If an inmate believes his legal rights have been infringed he should consider
consulting a solicitor or legal adviser at an early stage.

CASE STUDIES

Rudd Basho complains about racial discrimination

Rudd Basho has tried for several weeks to obtain a place on the Motor Mechanics
Vocational Training Course and has been placed on the waiting list. His probation
officer supports his application as he is serving his first custodial sentence in a
Young Offender Institution for taking and driving away (TADA) and has an obses-
sive interest in motor vehicles. Two vacancies arise and Rudd notices that both

vacancies are allocated to white youngsters and he feels he is being discriminated against. He makes a written complaint under the Request and Complaint system and receives an interim reply which states that the Race Relations Liaison Officer (RRLO) is investigating his complaint.

The RRLO investigates his complaint and is concerned to find that black youngsters are under-represented on the course. However, the youngsters who had waited longest on the waiting list were the ones who were offered the vacancies.

The RRLO responds along these lines on the form to Rudd but he feels aggrieved and frustrated about the situation. He decides to complete a Request and Complaint Appeal Form and this is sent to the Area Manager who asks for all the papers to be forwarded to him.

The Area Manager discusses the situation with the Governor before replying: 'I have carefully looked into your complaint claiming that you suffered racial discrimination over your application to attend the Motor Mechanics Vocational Training Course which is very popular and oversubscribed. I consider that your application was processed properly but share the RRLO's concern that non-white youngsters are under-represented. The Governor is addressing this issue as a matter of urgency. In view of your circumstances and the fact that your probation officer considers this course will help you address your offending behaviour, the Governor has decided that you should be given the next vacancy on the course.'

Rudd is pleased with the outcome on a personal level as the needs identified in his Sentence Plan are being addressed. In addition, the underlying imbalance and apparent unfairness is also being rectified.

Peter Miles appeals following the Restoration of Remission Board

Peter Miles is eligible to apply for restoration of remission. His application is carefully considered by the Board which is chaired by the Wing Governor. Peter is granted restoration of 28 days remission out of the 116 days which had been added to his sentence for disciplinary offences. Peter feels more days should have been restored and completes a Request/Complaint form:

'I wish to appeal against the Wing Governor's decision. His reasons for not giving me more are as follows:

"I have restored 28 days remission because you have kept clear of trouble for the past six months and this deserves to be recognised. I have taken into account your medical problems but feel you must make greater effort to find work."

'I do not agree with this and think it is unfair. I suffer with agoraphobia and this has made it difficult for me to find a suitable job. At my previous prison I worked as a wing cleaner and attended the gym every day. Since I've been at this prison I have gone to the gym every day and I help out on the wing from time to time and will continue to do so until a vacancy arises. I would like the other 30 days restored.'

The Governor replies:

'I have reviewed your case and would remind you that restoring added days is not an entitlement but a privilege that has to be earned. The decision about how many days to restore takes into account the nature of the disciplinary offences you committed, your overall performance based on the written reports compiled by staff together with your written application. You have had 116 days added to your sentence and are eligible to apply for a maximum of half to be restored. You are expected to behave and conform to prison rules throughout your sentence and that includes working regularly or attending educational classes. I am satisfied that the decision to restore 28 days was appropriate but generous in your case. In view of this your request for the restoration of further eligible days is refused.'

Paddy Naughtie receives a life sentence review

Paddy Naughtie received a mandatory life sentence 15 years ago for the murder of a night watchman during an armed robbery. The tariff for his offence was set at 18 years. Paddy recently had F75 reports completed on him and forwarded to Lifer Section in Headquarters. He has been expecting to receive a provisional release date reflecting his good progress in open conditions and involvement in the Community Service programme. Instead he receives a reply which informs him that he will remain at his current establishment.

Paddy Naughtie is very disappointed and completes a *Request/Complaint Form* in order to appeal against the decision. This is forwarded directly to Headquarters as it is a reserved subject, and he awaits a reply.

After four weeks he has not received a reply and arranges to see the Chairman of the Board of Visitors under Prisoner's Confidential Access. The chairman is sympathetic to Paddy and decides to contact Headquarters personally and expedite a reply which arrives the following week.

The reply from Headquarters explains fully their reservations and the reasons for his remaining in open conditions. However the reply offers some hope of an early F75 review as they have stated that after 12 months they will consider requesting progress reports.

While Paddy is disappointed at this setback he feels that if he successfully addresses issues surrounding his offending behaviour he will be considered for release on licence.

Nicola Harrington has a baby in prison

Nicola Harrington is six months pregnant and has been sentenced to 18 months imprisonment for theft. She is very angry about being sent to prison as she thought that the courts would be sympathetic to her situation and place her under the supervision of the Probation Service who she thought would be obliged to help her get a flat from the Council. She realises she will be still be serving her sentence when the baby is due to be born and gets very frustrated and vents her anger on prison staff. All attempts to calm her down and reason with her fail and in the weeks following sentence she commits several offences against discipline including damaging her cell furniture, abusing staff, disobeying orders and finally she assaults a female officer by punching her in the face. She is punished for this offence and has 42 days added to her sentence. Concern is expressed about the disruptive effect her behaviour will have on other mothers in the mother-and-baby unit. The Governor convenes a case conference where prison staff and professional colleagues reluctantly come to the conclusion that her disruptive behaviour is likely to seriously upset the smooth running and safe environment of the mother-and-baby unit. This means that she will not be able to keep her baby with her in prison after she has given birth. Nicola has no relatives or friends able to provide care, so arrangements are made with the Social Services Department to place the baby with foster parents after it is born. Nicola makes a formal complaint under the Request and Complaint system to the Area Manager against the Governor's refusal to admit her to a mother-and-baby unit, as this is a reserved subject. The Area Manager carefully considers her appeal and agrees to allow her to be admitted to the mother-and-baby unit but imposes strict conditions including a condition that she sign a compact with the prison promising to be of good behaviour. Nicola finally realises that her disruptive behaviour is not achieving anything and tearfully agrees to these conditions. The birth goes ahead and fortunately for all concerned Nicola keeps her side of the agreement and for now settles down to motherhood.

CHECKLIST

- When is it necessary for a prisoner to discuss a problem with the landing officer?
- How is an application made to the Governor?
- What is the formal time limit during which a matter must be raised?
- What is confidential access?
- How many complaints can an inmate have outstanding at any one time?

- What is a reserved subject under the Request/Complaint system?
- Who deals with reserved subjects?
- If a prisoner remains dissatisfied after receiving a formal reply, what is the appeal process?
- At what stage can a prisoner write to the Prisons Ombudsman?
- Can the Prisons Ombudsman investigate any aspect of a prisoner's treatment in custody?

- When should a prisoner seek legal advice?
- How is a petition made to the European Commission of Human Rights?
- When is it appropriate to involve an outside organisation with a problem?
- Is a prisoner entitled to seek compensation from the Prison Service?
- How should a prisoner proceed if he does not receive a reply from Headquarters within six weeks?

DISCUSSION POINTS

1. Examine the advantages and disadvantages of making a complaint using prisoner's confidential access.

2. Prisoners rely heavily on prison staff to help them with their needs and this inhibits them from complaining. To what extent is this comment valid?

3. 'Prisoner's rights will only be safeguarded when there are legally enforceable minimum standards in establishments.' Discuss.

4. Consider whether the Prisons Ombudsman's role would be more effective if he had executive power to interfere with decisions made by the Prison Service.

5. Examine how far the erosion of the Boards of Visitors' powers undermines their 'watchdog' role.

6. 'The introduction of an enforceable time limit regarding the submission of Request/Complaint forms is likely to deny prisoners justice.' Discuss.

CHAPTER 6

Prison Discipline

APPRECIATING THE LEGAL FRAMEWORK

The authority for taking any internal disciplinary action against an inmate is vested in the Prison Rules 1964 and the Young Offenders Institution Rules 1988.

Following the disturbances at HMP Manchester in 1990 which led to an enquiry under Lord Justice Woolf a new offence of Prison Mutiny was added, which is a criminal offence.

The Prison Security Act 1992 (Section 1) defines the offence as follows:

There is a prison mutiny where two or more prisoners, while on the premises of any prison, engage in conduct which is intended to further a common purpose of overthrowing lawful authority in that prison.

A major incident occurs when the Governor loses control of the prison because property is extensively damaged, staff or prisoners are injured and Control and Restraint (C & R) staff are deployed. In these circumstances it is likely that a charge of Prison Mutiny will be brought. On conviction the maximum penalty is a further prison sentence of ten years or a fine or both.

The danger of getting caught up in any incident is real. Any inmate who remains in the vicinity when a disturbance is in progress may be regarded as a participant. The use of video is increasingly used by staff when incidents break out and can easily establish who was 'at the scene'.

DIFFERENT TYPES OF OFFENCES

Prison Rule 47 and Young Offender Rule 50 set out 22 offences against prison discipline which can be laid against inmates.

The charges range from very serious offences like hostage taking (Rule 47, paragraph 2) and escaping (Rule 47, paragraph 7), which are criminal offences, to minor infringements of the rules (Rule 47, paragraph 20 and Rule 47, paragraph 21), which simply states that any offence against 'good order and discipline' is punishable.

The full list of offences is as follows:

1. *Commits any assault*

   This applies to any intentional and unlawful use of force against another person.

   Adjudicators differentiate between offences where an officer is pushed or those where punches are thrown, and occasions where an offensive weapon is used. The Governor will consider the seriousness of any injuries sustained as this is an important factor in deciding whether to involve the police. The victim can also make a formal complaint to the police if he believes a criminal offence has been committed. Normally, if the offence would warrant a charge of grevious bodily harm being brought in the community, then the police will become involved and a prosecution may result. An assault charge makes no distinction between assaults against staff or other prisoners, although any assault against a member of staff is considered very serious.

2. *Detains any person against their will*

   This charge applies to a hostage-taker. Such an offence is always referred to the police for criminal proceedings and in practice is never forgotten by prison staff.

3. *Denies access to any part of the prison to any officer or any person (other than a prisoner) who is at the prison in order to work there*

   This charge covers instances where barricades occur but may also be used if an inmate prevents an officer intervening to break up a fight.

4. *Fights with any person*

   A fight occurs when there is an exchange of blows or when both inmates wrestle with each other and commit a mutual assault. Some fights turn out, on further investigation, to be assaults.

5. *Intentionally endangers the health or personal safety of others or, by their conduct, are reckless whether such health or personal safety is endangered*

   Tampering with the mains supply in order to wire up a radio or other electrical item is a common example of this offence.

6. *Intentionally obstructs an officer in the execution of his/her duty – or any person (other than a prisoner) who is at the prison in order to work there – in the performance of his/her work*

   This normally means causing a physical obstruction but can also apply if an inmate deliberately provides false information to an officer.

7. *Escapes or absconds from prison or from lawful custody*

   The definition of an escape is when a physical obstacle has to be overcome such as the perimeter wall or fence. Absconds occur when inmates in open conditions abuse trust by going off limits, or fail to return to the establishment by an agreed time.

8. *Fails to comply with any condition under which he is temporaily released under rule 6 of these rules*

   This relates to the specific conditions included on the licence issued to cover a period of temporary release.

8A. *Administers a controlled drug to himself or fails to prevent the administration of a controlled drug to him by another person*

This charge is brought when an inmate fails a Mandatory Drug Test, and covers the period 30 days prior to the date of the test. In practice it is difficult for an inmate to argue that the drug was administered without their knowledge, for instance, that their coffee was spiked by another inmate for a joke, unless they can produce corroborative evidence to support their case. The onus is on all inmates to ensure they do not test positive. Cannabis remains in the body for up to 30 days and is not affected by any drugs prescribed in custody. Opiates only remain in the body for three days and the test can be affected by certain prescribed drugs, which is the reason the Medical Officer has to send a statement to the Governor listing any medication prescribed to the inmate during the previous 30 days preceding the Mandatory Drug Test.

The penalties for positive tests are generally much higher for opiates. A not guilty plea necessitates carrying out a second confirmatory drug test at the laboratory. This incurs additional costs and wastes time and if the inmate is subsequently convicted the punishment may be up to 50 per cent higher than for a guilty plea. Since a judicial review of June 1998, all inmates who test positive for drugs must be issued with the sheet *Information for Prisoners Who Have Tested Positive for Drugs.*

8B. *Is intoxicated wholly or partly as a consequence of knowingly consuming any alcoholic beverage*

This is the more serious of two alcohol-related charges and applies if the behaviour exhibited is consistent with intoxication.

8C. *Knowingly consumes any alcoholic beverage other than any prescribed to him pursuant to a written order of the medical officer*

This is the less serious alcohol-related charge and relates to the consumption of alcohol which has not been prescribed.

9. *Has in his possession:*

a) any unauthorised article, or

b) a greater quantity of any article than he is authorised to have

(a)   This applies to an item an inmate has in possession which does not appear on the privilege list.

(b)   Often used when an inmate is suspected of engaging in illegal trading or baroning-type activities, and is associated with bullying.

10. *Sells or delivers to any person any unauthorised article*

This covers supplying drugs or the illicit trading of items which are not permitted in possesssion.

11. *Sells or, without permission, delivers to any person any article which they are allowed to have only for their own use*

This charge applies if another inmate lends out their personal radio or other permitted item. This is often associated with bullying, in the experience of staff.

12. *Takes improperly any article belonging to another person or to a prison*

This charge is the equivalent to a charge of theft.

13. *Intentionally or recklessly sets fire to any part of a prison or any property, whether or not their own*

This applies to instances of arson.

14. *Destroys or damages any part of a prison or any property other than his own*
    This covers 'cell smash-ups', any damage to prison property, or intentional damage inflicted on another inmate's property.

15. *Absents himself from any place where he is required to be, or is present at any place where he is not authorised to be*
    Inmates who wander will generally be assumed to be up to no good. This causes staff extra work and some embarrassment, particularly if they cannot get the roll right.

16. *Is disrespectful to any officer or any person (other than a prisoner) who is at the prison in order to work there or any person visiting a prison*
    Inmates are committing an offence if they are rude to auxiliary staff, civilians, official visitors or the relatives of other prisoners.

17. *Uses threatening, abusive or insulting words or behaviour*
    The usual charge laid when inmates lose their temper, use bad language, or become abusive towards staff.

18. *Intentionally fails to work properly or, being required to work, refuses to do so*
    Any convicted inmate who refuses to work and is medically fit to carry out the required duties, is guilty of an offence.

19. *Disobeys any lawful order*
    It is not necessary for a member of staff to preface any instruction by the words 'I am giving you a direct order . . .' as some inmates mistakenly believe. Any polite request to carry out or refrain from doing something constitutes an order, providing it is reasonable and lawful.

20. *Disobeys or refuses to comply with any rule or regulation applying to him*
    The rule or regulation can be a local rule that only applies in a particular establishment. Provided reasonable steps have been made to inform inmates of the particular requirements, they are obliged to comply with them.

21. *In any way offends against good order and discipline*
    This is a 'catch-all' charge which is used when other paragraphs are not applicable.

22. *a) Attempts to commit,*
    b) Incites another prisoner to commit, or
    c) Assists another prisoner to commit or attempt to commit, any of the foregoing offences
    (a) applies if an attempt is made to commit any of the previous 21 charges;
    (b) persuading, making threats or applying pressure to others constitutes incitement;
    (c) covers active assistance.

ANSWERING CHARGES AT DISCIPLINARY HEARINGS

Disciplinary hearings are held by the Governor (or Controller in a privately run prison), on a daily basis, except Sundays and statutory or public holidays. The hearings are investigative, whereas the court system is adversarial. The Governor's primary role is to establish the facts, find out what really happened and the reasons for the breach of discipline (see Figure 6.1). The process must be conducted fairly with proper regard to the principles of natural justice and the Governor must be impartial. Hearings are

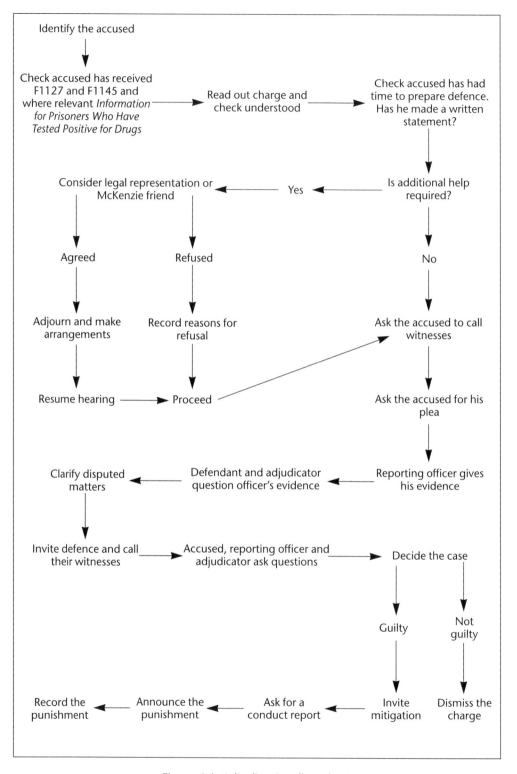

Figure 6.1: Adjudication flowchart

held as soon as practical and within 48 hours of the charge being discovered. Justice delayed is justice denied. 'Justice in prison (should be) secured through the exercise of responsibility and respect. The achievement of justice will itself enhance security and control' said Lord Justice Woolf in the *Woolf Report 1991*.

Being placed on Governor's report

Once the inmate has been isued with Form 1127 (see p. 168) he must be given a minimum of two hours to prepare his answer to the charge. Inmates charged under Rule 47(8a) must be issued with the sheet *Information for Prisoners Who Have Tested Positive for Drugs*.

Prior to the hearing the Medical Officer will examine the inmate and satisfy himself he is mentally fit to plead. If found guilty the Medical Officer has to be satisfied each inmate is physically fit to undergo punishment, particularly if a period of time in cellular confinement has been awarded by the Governor.

Following examination the Medical Officer signs a certification of medical fitness on Form F256, the *Record of Hearing and Adjudication* (see p. 170), which is where the adjudicating Governor makes a formal record of the hearing and outcome, including recording the punishment he decides is appropriate.

Although Governor's adjudications are a formal occasion they should be conducted in a relaxed atmosphere and inmates must be allowed to sit during the proceedings, and be given writing materials in order to make notes. Escorting staff sit either side of the inmate during the hearing, but are not allowed to face the inmate, known as 'eyeballing', during the proceedings. This practice is intimidatory and inhibits the accused when conducting his defence. If this does occur, it is grounds for complaint to the Area Manager under the Request and Complaint system, and the adjudication will be quashed under Prison Rule 56(1). The procedure at the adjudication is laid out on Form 1145, *Explanation of Procedure at Disciplinary Charge Hearings*, which is given to the inmate at the same time as Form 1127.

If an inmate pleads guilty to the offence, the reporting officer reads out the evidence from Form F254, *Report to the Governor of Alleged Offence by Inmate* (see p. 169), and the accused is given the opportunity to question the evidence or comment upon it. Inmates may call witnesses to corroborate their version of events. If a written answer to the charge is made this will be read out during the hearing and the inmate may be asked questions by the Governor.

Mitigating circumstances

Once the Governor is satisfied that the charge has been proved *beyond any reasonable doubt* then he will invite the inmate to make a plea of mitigation. This provides an opportunity for any explanation for their poor behaviour to be considered, or for relevant family or medical problems to be highlighted.

Inmates pleading guilty may find it preferable and advantageous to make a statement of mitigation on the back of Form 1127.

Conduct reports

Following the plea of mitigation, a member of staff from the Segregation Unit will read out a conduct report which has been prepared by wing staff. It will explain to the

Governor how the accused has behaved and co-operated with staff while in custody. However, the wing report must not comment on any previous convictions or refer to any previous periods of custody served.

Responding to the charge

If a not guilty plea is entered the reporting officer will read out a statement and the inmate will be given the opportunity to ask questions or comment on the evidence. The Governor will question the officer and any witnesses he calls to support his account of what happened.

The accused can reply to the charge and call any witnesses for the defence. Normally witnesses will be invited to appear, if willing to attend, and if they have a relevant contribution to make to the hearing. The Governor has discretion to withhold permission to call any witnesses he thinks are unnecessary, particularly if he believes the accused is acting unreasonably or considers the evidence is irrelevant or not in dispute.

Once all the witnesses have appeared and the accused given the opportunity to question them, the inmate has a further opportunity to say anything additional in his defence.

Once all the evidence has been heard, the Governor has to decide whether the charge has been proved beyond all reasonable doubt. He will listen to any mitigation the inmate wishes to be considered, then request a conduct report and decide on an appropriate punishment.

Refusing to appear

The hearing will proceed in the inmate's absence if he fails to co-operate by doing any of the following:

- by refusing to attend;
- by being indecently dressed;
- by being in a condition which is offensive to the adjudicator, for example on a dirty protest.

He will be advised that the hearing will go ahead in spite of his failure to co-operate. If this happens a not guilty plea will be entered, and the fact that the accused did not attend the hearing will be noted on the record of the hearing. The inmate will be advised of the outcome of the hearing, invited to offer any mitigation, then informed of the punishment.

Minor reports

A minor report system operates in Young Offender Institutions, but this can be extended to any prisoner under the age of 21, for offences of a less serious nature. The Governor can delegate this power to nominated senior staff (Principal Officers or above).

The process followed is a simplified version of the full adjudication procedure, but it must be conducted fairly and comply with the rules of natural justice.

The punishments that can be given to inmates if found guilty are limited to the following:

- a caution;
- three days' loss of specific privileges;
- three days' stoppage of earnings;
- extra work up to a maximum of six hours spread over three days.

An inmate has the right to appeal against any decision made on a minor report.

UNDERSTANDING INMATES' RIGHTS AND ENTITLEMENTS

Any inmate who feels unable to conduct his defence without assistance can request, when he attends the hearing, legal representation, or an adviser or friend, to be present.

Although inmates are entitled to request a solicitor to represent them, this facility is rarely granted nowadays. The level of disciplinary awards has been reduced since the Board of Visitors (BoV) were removed from the internal disciplinary process. At one time the BoV could impose a punishment of 180 additional days, equivalent to a further twelve months sentence before remission is taken into account. Governor's powers, while more limited, are significant; an additional 42 days is equivalent to a three months sentence in the local Magistrates' Court.

Grounds for legal representation

Any one of the following criteria must be fully satisfied before the Governor will approve a request for legal representation:

1. The seriousness of the charge and the potential penalty.
2. If any points of law are likely to arise.
3. The ability of the inmate to present his case.
4. Whether there are likely to be procedural difficulties.
5. The need for reasonable speed in completing the adjudication.
6. The need for fairness between prisoners and prison staff, particularly when there are several co-accused.

If legal representation is granted the case will be adjourned to enable the inmate to arrange to brief his solicitor.

A request to seek legal advice is normally considered favourably and the hearing adjourned to allow this to happen.

A further option is for an inmate to request the assistance of an adviser or friend, often referred to as a *McKenzie man*. His role is to take notes and offer advice, but he is not entitled to take part in the proceedings or speak on behalf of the accused unless invited to by the Governor.

Sanctions available to the Governor

The range of punishments available to the Governor is as follows:

1. A caution.
2. Loss of privileges for a maximum of 42 days (21 days if under 21).
3. Stoppage of earnings for up to 42 days (21 for those under 21).
4. Cellular confinement for up to 14 days (7 days for under-21s).
5. Up to a maximum of 42 added days to the sentence.
6. Removal from work for up to 21 days (adults only).

In addition, young offenders can be punished as follows:

1. Removal from activities for a maximum of 21 days.
2. Two hours extra work for up to 21 days.
3. Removal from the wing for up to 21 days.

More than one punishment can be awarded for a single offence but any punishment can be suspended for up to six months. Anyone serving a punishment of cellular confinement must be kept in a cell that has access to sanitary facilities at all times and contains a bed, bedding, a table and a stool or chair as a minimum.

Governors are obliged to have a local tariff for each offence which sets out the range of penalties for particular offences within their establishment, in order to ensure consistency between different adjudicating governors.

Conducting the defence

An adjudicator must be *satisfied beyond reasonable doubt* that an offence has been committed and an important element to establish is *intent*. A sustainable defence to certain charges is ignorance of a local regulation or that the incident was accidental. Self-defence is a complete defence to certain charges. The Governor will test out the validity of any defence offered before reaching his verdict.

The following are reasonable and sustainable defences to offer to each of the charges that can be laid under Rule 47:

Para. 1	Did the inmate actually use force, and if so, was it accidental or used in self-defence?
Para. 2	Was collusion a factor or did the inmate detain the victim against his will?
Para. 3	Was access denied to a member of staff intentionally?
Para. 4	Did the inmate believe the force used was lawful because he was acting in self-defence?
Para. 5	Was anybody else endangered by the actions of the accused?
Para. 6	Could the obstruction of a member of staff occur accidentally?
Para. 7	Was the inmate legally held in custody or did he have permission to leave the establishment?
Para. 8	Did the inmate fail to comply with a specific condition included on the

licence, or did he have a valid reason for non-compliance? In the case of sickness, did a doctor sign a statement confirming the inmate was unfit to travel?

Para. 8A   Can the inmate demonstrate the drug was lawfully prescribed to him or that it was administered to him under duress?

Para. 8B   Was the inmate intoxicated as a result of knowingly taking an alcoholic drink?

Para. 8C   Is the evidence about the inmate's observed behaviour consistent with consuming an alcoholic drink or is there some other plausible explanation?

Para. 9   Are the following three elements fully satisfied:
    (a)   *presence:* the article exists and can be produced;
    (b)   *knowledge*: the inmate knew it was where it was discovered;
    (c)   *control*: the offending article was owned by the accused and was under their personal control.

Para. 10   Did the inmate believe the article was authorised?

Para. 11   Was the inmate aware that the article was not allowed for his sole use?

Para. 12   Was the article taken intentionally and improperly, and did the accused exercise actual physical control over the item in question?

Para. 13   Was the inmate reckless?

Para. 14   Did the inmate own the item or believe it belonged to him?

Para. 15   Was the inmate aware of the requirement, or did the accused genuinely believe he had permission?

Para. 16   Are any of the following conditions satisfied:
    (a)   disrespect occurred and was directed towards somebody;
    (b)   the inmate was joking and had no intention of being disrespectful;
    (c)   the object of the disrespect was another prisoner.

Para. 17   The inmate, while being annoying or rude, did not intend to be abusive, insulting or threatening.

Para. 18   Although the inmate did not actually refuse to work his actions amounted to such a refusal. Had the accused completed the quota of work allocated for the day?

Para. 19   Did the inmate fail to comply with a lawful order by a member of staff?

Para. 20   Was the inmate made aware of the local rule or did he genuinely believe it did not apply to him?

Para. 21   Is the charge being used as a way of finding the accused guilty on less evidence than might otherwise be necessary?

Para. 22   Did the inmate intend to actively assist another prisoner to commit an offence?

RESTORATION OF REMISSION

A punishment can be terminated or reduced once awarded by the Governor (or Controller if accommodated in a private prison), if he feels it has achieved some good and is unlikely to be repeated. Alternatively, his decision may be based on medical advice from the Medical Officer.

In the case of added days he cannot alter the award once it has been implemented, but after six months an inmate may be eligible to be considered for restoration of remission. In a Young Offender Institution the qualifying period is four months.

Every inmate will have to demonstrate there has been a sustained improvement in his behaviour in the intervening period. Consideration for restoration of remission is made by making a written application to the Governor. Discipline staff will be asked to attach their written comments, which will normally be shown to the inmate. The Governor is only permitted to restore a maximum of half the days awarded as additional days.

Once the Governor has reached a decision on the application, the inmate must be informed in writing, and given the reasons for the decision within seven days.

An inmate can re-apply every six months provided he still remains eligible; they must not have appeared at a subsequent disciplinary hearing where further days have been added to their sentence, or added days have been activated for a previous suspended offence.

'RULE 43'

Segregation under Prison Rule 43 can take two forms:

1. *For an inmate's own protection*
   Any inmate may request to be segregated because of the nature of his offence or because he has been threatened or attacked by other prisoners and is in danger. Such a request has to be made in writing and submitted to the Governor for authorization.
2. *For the good order and discipline of the establishment*
   If an inmate's behaviour is considered to be subversive, or he is being disruptive or causing harm to others, the Governor can segregate him initially for up to three days.

Understanding the consequences of Rule 43 GOAD

Once an inmate has been placed on Rule 43 GOAD he is given a written statement by the Governor outlining why he has taken this action. The Governor will complete a form which is his legal authority for authorising segregation and will invite the Board of Visitors, if appropriate, to extend the period of segregation for up to 28 days. Thereafter it can be extended for further periods of 28 days by the BoV if the Governor so requests.

Segregation eventually may result in a transfer to another establishment, when it becomes clear that the individual is not going to be able to be returned to normal location on a wing. If a move is unavoidable prison staff are usually careful to ensure that such a move is not seen as a reward for bad behaviour. Often the effect is that an inmate moves further away from his home town, which makes it more inconvenient for the family to visit.

Periods spent segregated are recorded on the F2050 (the inmate case record), and invariably affect the level of regime and amount of privileges inmates enjoy. In addition, for many inmates eligible for parole, the circumstances will be brought to the attention of the Parole Board.

The danger is that an unsettled period in an inmate's sentence can be quite serious and have long-lasting effects. However, a sustained period of good behaviour can cancel out the ill-effects.

VIOLENT BEHAVIOUR

If an inmate becomes violent, staff are permitted to use force to control him in a number of ways:

1. *The use of the Special Cell*
   This includes replacing normal prison clothes with a canvas suit.
2. *By applying a variety of mechanical restraints:*
   (a) handcuffs;
   (b) a body belt;
   (c) leather ankle straps.
3. *Control and restraint techniques*
   This is the approved method used by prison staff to control violent prisoners. It involves the use of a three-man team to deal with each unco-operative individual and is widely accepted by inmates to be extremely effective as it involves the application of controlled pain to gain co-operation.

USING THE APPEALS SYSTEM

If an inmate feels dissatisfied with the outcome of an adjudication or believes the hearing was conducted unfairly, he is entitled to seek redress. There are several avenues open for complaint:

1. Appeal to the Area Manager using the Request and Complaint system: he has authority on behalf of the Secretary of State under Prison Rule 56(1) and YOI Rule 59(1) to quash any finding of guilt, or terminate or mitigate any award. This means fully stating the grounds of the complaint in writing; it may be the defence offered was not considered properly or the punishment was excessive. This will be sent to the Area Manager in Headquarters and he will normally ask for the Governor's written comments and to see the written record of the hearing. If he is not satisfied that the hearing was conducted properly he can exercise the delegated powers of the Secretary of State and either alter or quash the original decision.
2. The Prisons Ombudsman will consider an inmate's complaint if he remains dissatisfied with the Area Manager's review of the case. He will investigate the complaint and scrutinise the documentation and if he finds in favour of the inmate he can recommend that the finding of guilt is quashed or the punishment modified. He can be contacted at the following address: The Prison Ombudsman, Ashley House, 2 Monck Street, London SW1P 2BQ.
3. Inmates can seek leave to apply for judicial review. This means that the case is considered by a Judge in the Queen's Bench Division at the High Court. This can only be pursued if the inmate contacts his solicitor and asks him to apply for an order of

centiorari, which allows the Divisional Court to review the decision. There is no guarantee that a judge will be willing to review a case and in practice this is extremely rare.

4. If an inmate believes there has been a breach of the European Convention of Human Rights the case can be referred to the European Commission of Human Rights and on to the European Court of Human Rights for judgment, once all other avenues of redress have been exhausted.

Finally, each prison library contains a copy of the Prison Discipline Manual which all inmates are entitled to consult. It can be purchased from: Home Office Library, 55 Queen's Anne Gate, London SW1H 9AT.

CASE STUDIES

Rudd Basho refuses to work

Rudd is depressed because the mother of his girlfriend Lola has been admitted to hospital with terminal cancer and Lola is very distressed and contemplating taking her life. Rudd has become so overwhelmed with his problems that he cannot face going to work and coping with other inmates. He refuses an order to go to work and is moved to the segregation unit pending adjudication.

His Conduct Report confirms that his behaviour is normally good and this offence is out of character. The Governor is sympathetic to his situation and refers him to the Probation Officer for help. He imposes a nominal fine and suspends the award for one month. (The effect is that the punishment does not take effect unless Rudd commits another similar offence within one month.)

Peter Miles is discovered with a smoking device

Peter is found with an unauthorised article in his cell, namely a smoking device normally used for taking controlled drugs. He admits the offence and explains he uses it purely for relaxation purposes.

His conduct report reveals it is his first disciplinary report and he normally works well and co-operates fully with staff. The Governor imposes the standard level of punishment for that type of offence. The fact that Peter is serving five years for drug-related offences is irrelevant.

Paddy Naughtie assaults another inmate

Paddy assaults another inmate serving a short period of imprisonment allegedly because he has been 'wound-up' by the victim. The victim refuses to give evidence at the hearing for fear of being labelled a 'grass' but his injuries are significant; he has sustained severe bruising and cuts to his face and neck.

Paddy's conduct report shows that over the past 15 years there is a pattern of behaviour that demonstrates he is short-tempered and he has assaulted several other inmates. The Governor is unable to impose additional days to his sentence but imposes a hefty forfeiture of privileges and points out the effect of this offence.

It will be reflected in the progress reports staff write for the Parole Board who regularly review his circumstances and response in custody, and who consider whether he is suitable to be released on licence.

Nicola Harrington appeals against her punishment

Nicola Harrington is charged under Rule 47 paragraph 1 with assaulting an officer by punching her in the mouth, an offence witnessed by another member of staff. Nicola's defence is that she was provoked but there is no evidence to support this claim. The Governor finds the charge against her proved beyond any reasonable doubt. In mitigation Nicola explains her angry outburst is because a miscarriage of justice has occurred and that she should have been placed on probation, not sent to prison. The Governor listens to a conduct report on her which describes her as disruptive. It points out that already in this sentence she has three disciplinary offences recorded against her, namely abuse to staff, disobedience and damaging her cell furniture. In view of the serious nature of the offence the Governor awards 42 added days, the maximum penalty. Nicola appeals against the severity of the punishment to the Area Manager using the Request and Complaint procedure. He reviews the case carefully and concludes that the adjudication has been conducted fairly and that under the circumstances the maximum award is appropriate. Nicola continues to feel aggrieved and complains to the Prisons Ombudsman who investigates her complaint thoroughly, raising queries with both the adjudicating Governor and the Area Manager. He concludes by upholding the original award on the grounds that it is consistent with the tariff for such offences in the establishment and is appropriate in view of her poor disciplinary record in custody.

CHECKLIST

- How soon does a disciplinary hearing have to be held?
- How much time is given to an inmate to prepare his defence to a charge?
- Can an inmate insist on any witnesses attending the hearing?
- Under what circumstances should an inmate request a McKenzie man?

- Are inmates permitted to cross-examine the reporting officer during the hearing?
- What are mitigating circumstances?
- What cannot be referred to in an inmate's conduct report?

- What constitutes reasonable grounds for an appeal?
- Have the Board of Visitors jurisdiction in disciplinary matters?
- Can the Governor remit part of the punishment he has awarded?
- How long must elapse before an inmate is eligible to apply for added days to be restored?

DISCUSSION POINTS

1. Discuss the case for appointing an independent adjudicator to be involved in hearing the most serious disciplinary offences.

2. Identify the difference between administrative action and disciplinary action that the Governor may take.

3. Do you consider there are sufficient safeguards in the process of placing prisoners on Rule 43 GOAD? How do they gain redress if they feel unfairly treated?

4. Why are prisoners allowed to hear their conduct reports read out at a disciplinary hearing but are not permitted to see their personal case record?

5. Should there be minimum disciplinary awards for certain serious offences to ensure consistency?

CHAPTER 7

Respecting Racial and Religious Differences

THE RACE RELATIONS DIMENSION

Good relationships between different ethnic groups depend on everyone adopting a tolerant, fair approach, which is based on mutual respect.

Racial prejudice occurs when bias, intolerance or fear are present, and others form an opinion about an inmate with only a minimal amount of information available.

Holding a stereotype view is when decisions and judgments made are based on the mistaken assumption that all members of a racial group act in a predetermined way.

The Race Relations Act 1976 makes it unlawful for anybody to treat any inmate less favourably than anyone else on racial grounds, and calls this direct discrimination. If an inmate experiences less favourable treatment than someone else because of the colour of his skin, his race, nationality or ethnic origins, then he has suffered direct discrimination. Indirect discrimination is when the way individuals are treated results in unfairness.

Direct institutional discrimination happens if an ethnic group is not allowed to attend a particular class, or undertake a specific type of work. Indirect institutional discrimination is more subtle, but can arise for instance, if the Prison Shop fails to provide any of the toiletries requested by ethnic minority groups.

The Prison Service is publicly committed to good race relations and requires the *Race Relations Policy Statement* to be displayed at the main gate, in the visits room, in reception, and on wing notice boards. The *Race Relations Liaison Officer* (RRLO) monitors the ethnic mix, and checks that all inmates have the opportunity to take part in all available activities. He can help inmates by offering advice about problems of a racial nature, and has a list of contacts in outside agencies who can be approached for advice and assistance.

THE RACE RELATIONS POLICY STATEMENT

The Prison Service completely revised its policy statement on Race Relations in 1997, extending it to include religious discrimination:

> The Prison Service is committed to racial equality. Improper discrimination on
> the basis of colour, race, nationality, ethnic or national origins, or religion is

unacceptable, as is any racially abusive or insulting language or behaviour on the part of any member of staff, prisoner or visitor, and neither will be tolerated.

The Race Relations Policy Statement is based on nine standards which are as follows:

1. The policy statement has to be prominently displayed throughout the establishment.
2. Regular meetings of the Race Relations Management Team must take place.
3. A Race Relations Liaison Officer has to be appointed.
4. A Race Relations Audit has to be conducted annually and the results sent to Headquarters.
5. The ethnic origin of all inmates has to be recorded on reception.
6. Systems have to be introduced which ensure discrimination does not occur.
7. All racial incidents or complaints have to be recorded and investigated by the RRLO.
8. A list of contacts in outside agencies has to be kept.
9. Information and local training for all staff has to be provided.

ETHNIC MONITORING

One of the tasks of the Race Relations Liaison Officer (RRLO) is to carry out ethnic monitoring throughout the establishment. This is to ensure all inmates are treated fairly and that racial imbalances are not occurring. Ethnic monitoring is not intended to give anybody special treatment, as positive discrimination is equally unhealthy and causes resentment. The aim is to make sure everyone has an equal opportunity to take part in all activities, and to use the available facilities.

Ethnic monitoring makes checks on decisions that are made, and includes the following areas:

- inmates' categorisation and allocation;
- the accommodation they are allocated;
- the opportunity they have to attend work, education and training, with particular attention being paid to the most attractive jobs, such as work in the kitchen and 'red-bands' (positions of trust allocated to carefully vetted inmates);
- the disciplinary system;
- their suitability for release on licence;
- the proportion of ethnic prisoners and young offenders who are placed on the basic regime or held in the segregation unit;
- the Request and Complaints system.

ENSURING FAIR TREATMENT

It is every inmate's right to have an equal opportunity to take part in all work and educational, training, recreational and other amenities that are available in the establishment.

Problems and misunderstandings can easily arise if the special needs of minorities are not catered for, and the rights of others to practise their religious faith are not respected. Although religion is excluded from the scope of the Race Relations Act, acknowledging the ethnic needs of other faiths is an important part of healthy race relations.

Inmates can check they are being treated fairly in the following areas of prison life:

- Cells are being allocated on a rota basis, and no one racial group dominates a particular area. Nobody should refuse to share a cell with another prisoner on the grounds of his race or colour.
- The criteria for filling work and training vacancies should be on the basis of how well an inmate can do the job, or his need and aptitude for a particular training course.
- Education classes should be allocated after a careful assessment of educational need, which may mean providing special classes for those who have difficulty speaking English.
- The range of books and material available to read in the library should reflect all cultural interests. Foreign-language books should be available to borrow.
- According to Prison Rules, all food provided should be wholesome, nutritious, well prepared and served, reasonably varied and sufficient in quantity. In addition, consideration should be given to religious customs as well as cultural preferences, and vegetarian meals should be available as an option.
- The Prison Shop should stock vegan products, particularly food and toiletries, and provide hair and skin care items which meet the needs of ethnic minorities.
- If anybody offends against discipline they should be treated consistently by staff, and the same latitude extended to all prisoners. If an inmate is placed on report, the procedure followed and the punishment awarded should be identical to those of other ethnic groups. Any evidence of discrimination is grounds for an appeal, and will result in any finding of guilt being quashed.

MAINTAINING STANDARDS

Each establishment has to appoint a *Race Relations Management Team* (RRMT) which has the following responsibilities:

- to monitor the quality of race relations in the establishment;
- to identify and deal with race relations issues;
- to support the work of the Race Relations Liaison Officer;
- to advise the Governor about ways of developing good practice;
- to make sure that ethnic minority prisoners are being treated fairly and not experiencing any form of discrimination.

The RRMT must be chaired by a member of the Senior Management Team and include other senior managers, the Chaplain, the RRLO, a member of the Board of Visitors and a representative from a local community organisation. Ideally, the RRMT should include a representative prisoner on the committee, but if this is not possible, the RRLO has to make arrangements to consult with inmates, and find out their perception about the state of race relations locally.

The RRMT meets on a quarterly basis with the following terms of reference:

- to collect and examine ethnic monitoring data;
- to interpret developing trends;
- to audit performance;
- to form close links with relevant community-based organisations;
- to investigate any racial incidents;
- to provide training for all staff;
- to assist and support the RRLO to develop good practice;
- to provide regular reports to the Governor.

MAKING COMPLAINTS OF RACIAL DISCRIMINATION

Any complaint by an inmate which alleges racial discrimination is particularly sensitive, and is thoroughly investigated if raised through the normal Request and Complaints process.

The Race Relations Liaison Officer has a special role to play in each establishment, monitoring policy and practice. His job is to promote good race relations, liaise between staff and inmates, and make sure the Prison Service policy on Race Relations is being followed. If an inmate experiences any difficulties, or feels he is being treated unfairly on grounds of race, an approach to the RRLO in the first instance is the best course of action. He may be able to resolve a problem informally by talking to those involved, especially if the difficulty has been caused by a lack of understanding of an individual's ethnic needs.

All inmates are entitled to make a complaint to the Commission for Racial Equality, which can investigate complaints that contravene the Race Relations Act 1976. Any letters will be treated as confidential, and should be addressed to: Commission for Racial Equality, Elliot House, 10–12 Allington Street, London SW1E 5EH. Telephone 0171–828 7022.

FOLLOWING A RELIGIOUS FAITH

Each establishment appoints Ministers and Chaplains to help inmates follow their religious faith. Currently over 40 religious denominations are represented, and the Prison Service must make arrangements under the Prison Act 1952 to allow everyone the opportunity to practise their chosen religion. The prison has a responsibility to provide each faith with a room which is suitable to hold meetings and services.

Inmates are allowed holy books and religious items in their possession, and may attend the main service of the week. In addition they should have an opportunity for private prayer and meditation. Inmates are not automatically stopped from attending services because they are in the segregation unit undergoing punishment, or located in the prison hospital. The Governor has discretion to stop any inmates attending if he thinks they pose a security risk, or may be disruptive, or if the Medical Officer advises against them attending a church service.

The Chaplain or a Visiting Minister is obliged to visit inmates on a daily basis while undergoing punishment, or if they are ill in hospital. He will offer pastoral support, assist with any personal problems, particularly if an inmate suffers a bereavement, or a member of his family is involved in a serious accident. He also becomes involved if an inmate decides to apply to marry while in prison.

Inmates are not normally expected to work on their recognised day of religious observance, unless it is unavoidable. Some jobs have to be carried out on a daily basis, like cleaning, catering and feeding livestock. Everyone should be given an opportunity to attend any groups or classes that are being held, including Missions and Seminars.

When inmates arrive in prison they are asked about their religion, in order to register them and offer advice about the facilities available. If an inmate registers as 'nil religion' on reception, his wishes will be respected and he will not receive visits from ministers of religion. An inmate can apply to change his religion provided he obtains the Governor's consent. The Governor needs to be satisfied that the reasons are genuine, and not that an individual wishes to obtain some additional privilege; and will first consult the ministers involved before reaching a decision.

Christianity

Christians believe that God created the heaven and earth and that he sent his son Jesus Christ into the world. Mary, a virgin, gave birth to Jesus who was conceived by the Holy Spirit. He was crucified, died, and resurrected on the third day after his death, and later ascended to heaven where he will remain until he returns to judge the living and the dead. After the Ascension, Christians received the power of the Holy Spirit, and the church was born and developed worldwide. Christians believe in the Holy Spirit, the holy catholic church, the forgiveness of sins, the resurrection of the body, and in everlasting life. Over the centuries the church has divided into many denominations and includes the Roman Catholic Church, the Church of England, the Orthodox Churches and the Free Churches, which includes among others Baptists, Methodists, Pentecostals, Quakers, the Salvation Army and the United Reformed Church.

Arrangements must be made in prison for an inmate to have the option to attend Chapel on a Sunday. This weekly celebration of the resurrection is when the Holy Eucharist, Holy Mass, Holy Communion, or the Lord's Supper are celebrated. Chapel services are also held on Christmas Day, Good Friday and Easter Day. Ash Wednesday is celebrated as a Holy Day by Roman Catholics.

Christians believe that the writers of the Bible were inspired by God and treat it as sacred. The Old Testament contains the 39 Jewish Scriptures and the New Testament contains 27 books. These include the Gospels, about the life of Jesus, the Acts of the Apostles, about the early church, and Christian teaching and prophecy.

Inmates can pray and read the Bible in their cell, and attend the Chapel for worship each Sunday.

There is no special diet for Christians, although some fast during Lent, and Roman Catholics fast on Ash Wednesday and Good Friday.

Only Christian clergy and lay people participating in services wear any special clothing, although many Christians wear a cross, crucifix or use rosary beads.

The Chaplaincy team in a prison consists of the Church of England Chaplain, the Roman Catholic Chaplain and the Methodist Minister. Any other ministers appointed are called visiting ministers and they visit inmates of that specific denomination. All the appointed Chaplains will help anyone who wishes to practise their religion, and if requested, make contact with a religious leader of their own faith.

Baha'i

Balla'u'llah, the founder, teaches the oneness and wholeness of the human race, and emphasises the principles of equality and justice.

There are eleven holy days, and on two of these inmates are not required to work. These are the 'Feast of Naw-Ruz' on 21 March and the 'First Day of the Feast of Ridvan' on the 21 April. Inmates may observe the 'Nineteen Days Fast' which takes place between 2 March and 20 March and take their meals during the period of sunset and sunrise.

The Writings of Balla'u'llah form a large part of the Baha'i Scriptures which include prayers. A compilation of Baha'i Scriptures is available, called 'Inspiring the Heart'.

Private worship can take place in an inmate's cell, and a regular meeting of Baha'i followers should be possible. The Baha'i meeting should take place on the first day of each month in their 19-month year.

There are no special diet or dress requirements.

Further advice can be obtained by approaching: National Spiritual Assembly of the Baha'is of the United Kingdom, 27 Rutland Gate, London SW7 1PD. Telephone 0171–584 2566.

Buddhism

Buddhism is based on the teachings of Siddhartha Gotama, born in 623 BC, who became known as the 'One Who Knows' or The Enlightened One, or the Buddha. Buddhism is a philosophy rather than a religion, and Buddhists believe spiritual peace can be gained through willpower, self-discipline and lifestyle.

Inmates can celebrate the following three main festivals:

- Buddha Day in May;
- Dhamma Day in July;
- Sangha Day in October.

If the Buddhist Visiting Minister cannot attend, inmates should meet as a group in a suitable room.

The main scriptures are the 'Tripitaka', eight times longer than the Bible, the Drammapada, which is a collection of popular verses, and the Mahayana which is accepted as 'the Word of Buddha'.

Private worship is possible in a cell, and images of Buddha, rosaries and meditation stools are allowed in possession, but incense can only be used when the Visiting Minister comes in to lead meetings.

Inmates may have either a vegetarian diet, which excludes fish, or a vegan diet. There are no special dress requirements but work which involves the slaughter of animals must be avoided.

Further advice can be obtained by approaching: Angulimala, The Forest Hermitage, Lower Fulbrook, Warwick CV35 8AS. Telephone 01926–624385.

Chinese religion

There are four main strands to Chinese religion:

- *Shamanism*, popularly portrayed in Kung Fu films, where superhuman beings materialise from nowhere;
- *Taoism*, meaning The Way;
- *Confucianism*, which is more a philosophical system;
- *Buddhism*, which centres on salvation by offering intercession to bodhisattvas, who are enlightened beings.

The main festivals observed in establishments are as follows:

- *Chinese New Year*, when Chinese prisoners are excused work, and allowed to wear a red item of clothing;
- *Ching Ming*, the Festival of the Dead, which takes place on 5 April;
- *Dragon Boat Festival* in June;
- *Moon Festival* in September.

Chinese Buddhists read the *Lotus Sutra*, but the yearly Almanac, called the *T'ung Shu*, is an important document which followers hang by a red cord beside the door to keep evil forces at bay.

All worship is of a private nature, and there are no dress restrictions.

Further advice and guidance can be obtained from: International Consultancy on Religion, Education and Culture, Manchester Metropolitan University, 799 Wilmslow Road, Didsbury, Manchester, M20 8RR. Telephone 0161–434 8374.

Hinduism

Hinduism is an open religion, in that Hindus worship many manifestations of God, and believe in the doctrine of reincarnation. Hinduism can be described as a way of life rather than purely a religion.

Inmates are excused work to celebrate:

- *Holi* in February or March;
- *Diwali* in October or November;
- *Mahashivratri* in February or March;
- *Rama Navami* in March or April;
- *Janmashtami* in August or September;
- *Dussehra* or *Navoratri* in October.

The Bhagavad Gita, or Song of the Lord, is the sacred writing which is recommended reading.

Private worship is possible in a cell, but the Hindu Visiting Minister will wish to lead worship, usually on a Sunday. Washing facilities should be available for ritual washing.

Most Hindus are vegetarians, but none will eat beef as the cow is a sacred animal.

Some men may wear a *yagyopavit*, known as the Second Thread. Most women wear a *Sari* or Shalwar Kameez, and married women a *Bindi*, which is a coloured spot on the forehead.

Further advice and guidance can be obtained from the Official Consultant at: Institute of Indian Culture, 4A Castletown Road, London W14 9HQ. Telephone 0171–381 3086.

Islam (Muslim)

Islam stands for purity, peace, and complete submission and obedience to the will of Allah, who they claim to be the only God. Muslims believe in all the prophets, a Day of Judgment, and life after death.

The main festivals celebrated are:

- *Eid-al-Fitr*, which celebrates the ending of the Fast of Ramadan;
- *Eid-al-Adha*, the Festival of Sacrifice.

Inmates are not required to work on either day, and congregational prayers take place around 11 a.m. In some establishments it may be possible to celebrate these festivals by allowing food to be prepared and sent in by the Islamic Cultural Centre or the local Iman.

If the *Fast of Ramadan* is observed, which lasts for a lunar month, Muslims will be provided with sufficient food for two meals to be eaten after sunset and before dawn.

Other Holy Days include The Day of Hijrah, Meelad-un-nabi, Lailat-ul-Miraj and Lailat-ul-Qadr.

The *Holy Qur'an* or Koran is the sacred writing which reveals God's will for mankind through his prophet Mohammed.

Private worship is possible in a cell and involves saying prayers five times daily. Inmates need access to running water for ritual washing, the *Qur'an*, a prayer mat and a cap.

Group worship should take place under the leadership of the Iman, but if this is not possible, one of the inmate groups can act as prayer leader. This should take place each Friday between 1 p.m. and 2 p.m. in a suitable room which has access to washing facilities, and the floor should be covered with sheets.

Muslims are forbidden to eat pork. They may eat a vegetarian diet, a vegan diet, or an ordinary diet with halal meat and poultry provided as an option.

There are no special dress requirements, other than men cover their heads while praying, and women cover the whole body apart from their face and hands. Married women should wear wedding bangles or a taviz.

Further advice can be obtained from: The Islamic Cultural Centre, 146 Park Road, London NW8 7RG. Telephone 0171–724 3363.

Jainism

Jainism, which originated in India in 527 BC, is based on the teaching of Vardhamana Mahavira. Jains believe the soul can obtain liberation or Moksha by following the principles of Jainism. These are *ahimsa* (non-violence), *sanyam* (self-control), and *tap* (penance), which can be achieved by meditation, fasting and study.

Inmates can be excused work to celebrate the main festivals:

- *Divali* in late October or early November;
- *Mahavira Jayanti* in March or April;
- *Paryushana*, an eight-day fast, in August–September.

Their sacred writings were compiled at the Council of Valabhi in 450 AD. Inmates can conduct private worship in their cell; holding meetings is optional where images of the Jain sages, prayer beads and incense can be used. The visiting Jain Minister or an inmate member can lead group meetings.

Inmates should follow a vegetarian diet which omits eggs, fish, root crops, onions and garlic. There are no special dress requirements.

Further advice can be obtained by approaching: Jain Association of United Kingdom, Jain Centre, Oxford Street, Leicester LE1 5XU.

Judaism

The Jews believe there is only one God, who created and rules over the whole universe. God revealed the *Torah*, or law, which is the first five books of the Old Testament, to his chosen people, and has a special covenant relationship with them. Within Judaism there are three strands:

- *Orthodox Judaism*, which is the traditionalist approach. They believe the complete revelation of God's eternal will has been revealed through the Bible.
- *Conservative Judaism*, which focuses on the historical aspects of Jewish tradition, and emphasises modern Zionism, and the preservation of the 'people of Israel'.
- *Reform Judaism* is progressive and evolving. It concentrates more on ethical principles rather than strictly obeying the law.

Inmates are excused work on the Sabbath, which lasts from sunset on Friday until sunset on Saturday, and on the following major festivals:

- *Rosh Hashannah* or New Year;
- *Yom Kippur* or the Day of Atonement;
- *Sukkot* which is the Feast of Tabernacles and includes the Rejoicing of the Law;
- *Pesach* or Passover;
- *Shavuot* or Pentecost.

Arrangements will be made for inmates to observe the fast on the Day of Atonement, and the Visiting Minister may be allowed to bring in supplementary foods for Jews to celebrate Passover.

Sacred writings are the Holy Scriptures, the Authorised Daily Prayer Book, the Pentateuch and Haftorahs.

Private prayers are possible in a cell, including the wearing of *phylacteries* for morning prayers, a small cap known as a *yarmulke* or *kippah*, and a prayer shawl or *talith*, which they can keep in possession. The Visiting Minister will normally conduct services on the Sabbath.

Under certain circumstances kosher food may be provided for strict Jews, but Jews are not allowed to eat bacon or pork.

Further advice and guidance can be obtained from: United Synagogue Executive Offices, 735 High Road, London N12 0US. Telephone 0181–343 6262

Sikhism

Sikhs believe in one supreme God and follow the teaching of the ten Gurus. Their founder Guru Nanak was born in 1469.

Sikhism teaches the unity of God, the equality of all people, and that their duty is to do God's will and live peacefully with other people. A central belief is meditation and reincarnation.

Inmates may be excluded work on the following Holy Days:

- *Baisakki* (the Sikh New Year's Day, on 13 April);
- *Birthday of Guru Nanak,* the founder Guru, in November.

Other festivals Sikhs can celebrate are *Divali*, the Festival of Light, in October or November, and *Holy Mohalla* in February or March. The local Sikh community may bring inside *Kara Prashad*, a specially blessed sweetmeat, and *Langer*, a vegetarian meal, which play an important part in the celebrations of these festivals.

The Sikh holy books are the *Sacred Nit-Nem* and the *Guru Granth Sahib*.

Private devotions can take place in a cell provided there are facilities for symbolic washing. The visiting Sikh minister will lead group worship in a quiet room, and bring in *Kara Prashad* to eat during the service.

All Sikhs should follow a vegetarian diet, and not consume halal or kosher meat, or tobacco. There is no dress requirement for an apprentice Sikh, known as a *Saihajdhari*, but a baptised male Sikh, known as an *Amridhari*, should keep his hair long, wear a turban and observe the *Five K's* which represent spirituality.

The Five Ks are:

- *Kesh,* the hair is uncut including the beard.
- *Kangha*, a comb which is used to keep the hair in place.
- *Kirpan*, a sword or dagger originally carried as a means of protection and which symbolises dignity and respect. In prison only a symbolic kirpan is permitted, such as a small replica metal dagger inlaid into the comb.
- *Kachs*, which are short trousers worn by men and women.
- *Kara*, a steel bracelet worn on the right wrist.

Further advice and guidance can be obtained from: The Sikh Cultural Society, 88 Mollison Way, Edgware, Middlesex HA8 5QW. Telephone 0181–952 1215; or Sikh Youth Service, 49 Sycamore Road, Handsworth, Birmingham B21 0GZ. Telephone 0121–523 0147.

Church of Christ, Scientist (Christian Science)

The Church of Christ, Scientist was founded in 1879 by Mary Baker Eddy, and has 2400 branches worldwide. The church was formed 'to commemorate the Word and works of our Master, which should reinstate primitive Christianity and its lost element of healing'.

Christian Science celebrates the main Christian holidays and uses the Authorised Version of the Holy Bible. In addition believers should read *Science and Health* and *Christian Science Quarterly.*

Inmates can study the Bible, *Science and Health,* and the weekly Lesson Sermons in their cell, and meet for a service on Sundays with the Visiting Minister.

There are no dietary restrictions other than to abstain from tobacco; neither are there any dress requirements.

Further advice and guidance can be obtained from the: District Manager, Christian Science Committee on Publications, 2 Elysium Gate, 126 New Kings Road, London SW6 4LZ. Telephone 0171–371 0600.

The Church of Jesus Christ of Latter-day Saints (Mormon)

The Mormon Church was started in 1830 by Joseph Smith Junior following a vision. Mormons believe that man is created in the image of God, but reject the doctrine of original sin. They believe humans have immortal souls and the state of afterlife is decided by their response to good and evil in the world.

Sundays and the main Christian holidays are celebrated, and followers treat as sacred the King James version of the Bible and the Book of Mormon.

Inmates can have private devotions in their cell, and attend a service of worship with the Visiting Minister when possible. Mormons are encouraged to attend worship with other Christian denominations when that is not possible.

Tea and coffee are not permitted, but cocoa is allowed. Mormons should also abstain from tobacco. There are no dress requirements.

Further advice and guidance can be obtained from: The Area President, The Church of Jesus Christ of Latter-day Saints, 751 Warwick Road, Solihull, West Midlands B91 3QR. Telephone 0121–711 2244.

Jehovah's Witnesses

Jehovah's Witnesses believe that the Bible is the inspired word of God, but reject certain orthodox doctrines of Christianity concerning the Trinity, and do not accept that Jesus Christ is fully God. They believe that the Second Coming of Christ took place in 1914, and that the current turmoil on earth is evidence that the 'last days' are happening as prophesied by Jesus.

Jehovah's Witnesses do not celebrate any of the traditional festivals other than the death of Jesus on Nisan 14, that is late March or April, and hold a Memorial Service in the evening.

They treat the Bible as sacred, studying the New World Translation of the Holy Scriptures, and their periodicals *The Watchtower* and *Awake.* Inmates can study the Bible and *The Watchtower* in their cell, and group meetings can be held in any suitable room. The visiting Jehovah's Witness Minister will lead believers in study and prayers.

There are no special diet or dress requirements.

Further advice can be obtained from: Watch Tower House, The Ridgeway, London NW7 1RN. Telephone 0171–906 2211.

Seventh-day Adventism

The Seventh-day Adventist Church believe salvation can only be obtained through faith in Jesus Christ. They closely follow the Ten Commandments, observe the Saturday as the Sabbath, believe God forgives their sins, and stress the imminent return of Christ.

The Sabbath is treated as a Holy Day, and inmates are excused work from sundown on Friday until Saturday evening.

The Holy Bible is sacred and the writings of Ellen G. White published in 1860 are treated as inspired by God.

Private study and worship is possible in a cell, and group meetings can be led by ordained Ministers.

A vegetarian diet is recommended, and tobacco is forbidden.

Further advice and guidance can be obtained from: Seventh-day Adventists, South England Conference, 25 St John's Road, Watford, Hertfordshire WD1 1PY.

Veganism

Veganism is not a religion but a philosophy that rejects the exploitation of animals for food or clothing.

Veganism is a way of life, and a vegan chooses not to be involved in any sport, hobby, or trade that causes distress, harm or suffering to any animal. It follows that vegans may not wish to be employed in the kitchen or on the prison farm.

The vegan diet is based on fruit, vegetables, nuts, pulses and cereals. No animal products, including meat, fish, eggs, milk or honey can be eaten. This extends to toiletries containing any animal ingredients or items that have been tested on animals. Clothing and footwear must not contain wool, silk, leather or suede.

Further advice and guidance can be obtained from: The Vegan Society, Donald Wilson House, 7 Battle Road, St Leonards-on-sea, East Sussex TN37 7AA. Telephone 01424–427393.

Rastafarianism

Rastafarianism is not recognised by the Prison Service as a separate religion, because it is partly religious and partly political in nature. Rastafarianism started in Jamaica in the 1930s and followers believe the late Emperor Haile Selassie, *Ras Tafari*, acted as an intercessor between God and man.

Rastafarians are vegetarian, although it is acceptable to eat fish. Many wear their hair in dreadlocks and cover them with a *tam*. Rastafarians can keep their dreadlocks in prison, and will be allowed to wear a suitable hat to keep them tidy.

An area of difficulty is the use of Cannabis Sativa, often referred to as *ganga*, holy herbs or wisdom weed on religious grounds which is not permitted. However, reggae music, which is very popular with Rastafarians, can be enjoyed in custody.

CASE STUDIES

Rudd Basho registers as a Muslim

Rudd Basho is a single West Indian youngster sentenced to twelve months Youth Custody for taking and driving away vehicles. On arrival, he is seen by staff in Reception who ask him about his religion, and he informs them he is a Muslim. His religion is registered as Islam and he is advised of the arrangements for group worship. These take place in the multi-faith room each Friday between 1 p.m. and 2 p.m., and are led by the Iman.

Rudd requests a vegetarian diet, and the kitchen are notified of his preference. The kitchen are interested to know he is a Muslim, as he will wish to observe the Feast of Ramadan which lasts for a lunar month. This involves making preparations so Rudd can be provided with sufficient food, in suitable containers, for two meals to be eaten after sunset and before dawn.

Peter Miles is on punishment

Peter Miles is serving five years imprisonment for the illegal importation of Class A drugs, and for supplying them to young people. He was placed on closed visits following an incident when his common-law wife was observed on closed circuit TV passing him a small package. Later he had a Mandatory Drug Test which proved positive, and he was charged with a disciplinary offence. Now Peter has been found in possession of a quantity of heroin, and the punishment is 14 days cellular confinement with no privileges in the Segregation Unit. While undergoing punishment the Roman Catholic priest visits him each day, as he registered RC on first reception. He applies to attend the service in the Chapel on Sunday and the Governor agrees, as there is no reason to believe he will misbehave or pose a security risk.

Paddy Naughtie suffers a bereavement

Paddy Naughtie is a divorced man in his fifties, serving a life sentence for the murder of a night watchman while committing an armed robbery. He has no living relatives, apart from his mother who is in her eighties, terminally ill with lung cancer. Information is received that his mother has died, and the Chaplain is asked to see Paddy to break the news to him. The Chaplain verifies the details of his mother's death from the hospital, and learns that she died peacefully in her sleep, in the early hours of the morning. He sees Paddy and offers him counselling, conscious that he became very depressed when his father died two years previously. The Chaplain contacts Paddy's female friend concerning the funeral arrangements, and assists in making practical arrangements for him to attend the funeral.

Nicola Harrington requests a change of religion

Nicola Harrington is serving her second custodial sentence for shoplifting. She is anti-authority, unco-operative, and her poor behaviour has resulted in her being placed on the basic regime. On reception she registers as 'nil religion', but has now changed her mind. She applies to change her religion to Mormon, and the Governor consults the Chaplain for his advice. It emerges that the main reason for her request is that she has discovered Mormons do not drink tea or coffee, and she prefers cocoa, which is the approved alternative. Nicola is a heavy smoker, despite the fact that she has a very young baby and Mormons do not approve of smoking. Neither the Chaplain nor Mormon Minister believe her reasons are genuine, and the Governor declines her request.

CHECKLIST

- How would you ensure that all inmates know what facilities are available for them to practise their religion?
- What accommodation needs to be provided for group worship?
- Why should the Race Relations Management Team meet regularly?
- Are inmates represented on the RRMT?
- Can inmates of all religions have private prayers?
- Are items of religious significance permitted?

- How should the diet cater for the requirements of all religious faiths?
- Who ensures that an ethnic balance is maintained in allocations to work?
- How can the Prison Shop cater for the preferences of ethnic minorities?
- What action is taken when ethnic monitoring reveals an imbalance is occurring?

- Are inmates informed about local arrangements to observe festivals and holy days?
- What is a Vegan diet?
- Can special food be brought in to celebrate religious festivals?
- How can the library cater for the interests of ethnic minorities?

DISCUSSION POINTS

1. It is important to cater appropriately for the special needs of ethnic minorities, but to prevent positive discrimination. How can the correct balance be achieved?

2. What strategies should be adopted to prevent institutional discrimination?

3. Examine the arguments for and against having inmates represented on the Race Relations Management Team.

4. Muslims and Sikhs require that special food is prepared and brought inside to celebrate certain festivals. How can the needs of other faiths be balanced against the security risks?

5. 'Rastafarianism and Veganism should be recognised by the Prison Service as religions.' Discuss.

6. How can current arrangements be improved for inmates located in the Segregation Unit or Prison Hospital, who find it difficult to attend religious services?

CHAPTER 8

The Regime

HEALTH CARE

The health care standards that apply to inmates are identical to those the general public receive from the National Health Service.

All new receptions are examined by the Medical Officer within 24 hours of arrival and decisions made about the following:

- Any identified health care needs and treatment required.
- Suitability for normal location.
- Whether fit enough to work within the prison.
- Which is the correct employment classification including fitness to work in the kitchen. The Medical Officer decides on the appropriate work category for each inmate as follows:
    category 1 is heavy work;
    category 2 is medium work;
    category 3 is light duties only.
No one must take part in work of a heavier type than has been agreed and anyone unfit for work due to illness will be excused work completely.
- Fitness for physical education will be assessed as follows:
    Fit 1A means able to take part in the full range of activities;
    Fit 1B allows participation in a more restricted range of activities but excludes gymnastics involving apparatus, team games that involve bodily contact such as football, and weight-lifting competitions. A decision will be made about the need for remedial classes or whether an inmate is unfit for activities in the gym altogether.
- Any special physical or mental health needs, including the risk of suicide or self-harm.

A full range of Mental Health Services can be offered in Local Prisons and Remand Centres, including observation, assessment, treatment and mental health care on an in-patient basis. This may include transferring patients to an appropriate hospital under the Mental Health Act 1983 if they are suffering with a severe and psychotic mental illness. If they need to be admitted to the prison hospital the regime provided should include educational classes, occupational therapy and an opportunity to take part in communal or leisure activities. The regime should be based on a multi-disciplinary therapeutic approach, with visiting specialists, involvement from the Health Authority and Social Service staff.

Anybody exhibiting challenging behaviour should be given appropriate medication and only placed in a secluded place or forcibly restrained as a last resort. Medication is adminstered contrary to a patient's wishes, only if he is in a life-threatening condition or to prevent him or others coming to serious harm. Under these circumstances two doctors would authorise it in writing, one of whom would be an *approved doctor* under Section 12 of the Mental Health Act 1983.

Health care is provided on a 24-hour basis for out-patients with a Medical Officer on call. A full range of primary care services is available and is similar to the service provided in general practice. Under the Access to Health Records Act 1990 an inmate is entitled to see his health records.

The following services are available:

- consultations and medical investigations;
- referral to external specialist services and clinics;
- undertaking minor surgical procedures;
- contraceptive services;
- ante-natal and post-natal care;
- counselling;
- dental and optical services;
- health care educational presentations on matters relating to the prevention of coronary heart disease and strokes, cancers, stress, sexually transmitted diseases, drug addiction and HIV/AIDS.

KEEPING FIT

Physical education (PE) is an important part of the prison regime which is popular and valued by most inmates. It improves the quality of life by helping them to keep fit and by countering the damaging effects of inactivity and boredom. PE programmes try to promote a healthy lifestyle and cater for physical fitness needs. They should cater for all ability levels and interests including providing outdoor activities. Achieving personal goals is important and this can be facilitated by taking part in competitive sporting activities, which encourages team working and the development of leadership skills.

The PE programme should run every day and provide opportunities for inmates to attend weekend and evening sessions. Suitable clothing should be provided and each class should last for at least an hour, including time for showering and getting changed. Convicted adults can attend a minimum of one session a week, Young Offenders at least two sessions weekly and juveniles can have a minimum of five hours a week in the gym. Twice a year everyone can have a personal fitness assessment test.

While all activities must comply with Health and Safety legislation, inmates should appreciate that there is a degree of risk involved in PE activities. The Central

Council of Physical Recreation's Charter of Fair Play is the standard that applies in the Prison Service, and all risks must thus be assessed and minimised, the equipment used has to be kept in good working order and PE programmes supervised by qualified staff.

The PE programme aims to achieve the following:

- provide constructive activity and prevent boredom;
- increase self-confidence and self-esteem;
- improve physical health and fitness;
- gain qualifications which may improve employment prospects;
- establish positive links with the local community;
- encourage inmates to show consideration for others and act responsibly;
- assist in preparation for release.

The PE programme should provide certification of external award schemes and assist in the following areas:

- *Lifestyle PE*
  This is using leisure time wisely, enjoying taking part in sporting activities and adopting a healthy lifestyle.
- *Self-esteem*
  This can be enhanced by learning new skills, tackling new challenges and gaining externally validated sports awards.
- *Social responsibility*
  Becoming involved in community projects and taking part in sporting events with outside teams can give inmates the oportunity to demonstrate the ability to act responsibly.
- *Social skills*
  The PE programme encourages inmates to develop tolerance, social skills and self-discipline.
- *Remedial exercise*
  The Medical Officer can use PE to help with a medical condition or difficulty.
- *Employment training*
  The opportunity exists to gain skills and qualifications essential for employment in the leisure industry.

A wide range of activities is available which can help meet these objectives, including football, rugby, cricket, basketball, weight-lifting and training, volleyball.

GAINING A PHYSICAL EDUCATION QUALIFICATION

An inmate who is interested in physical education may be able to develop his potential to the point where he decides to work in the leisure industry on release.

A basic qualification is the Community Sports Leadership Award; this may be followed by the National Vocational Qualification (NVQ) in Sport and Recreation (see Figure 8.1) which covers a wide range of activities and is available at Levels 1–4.

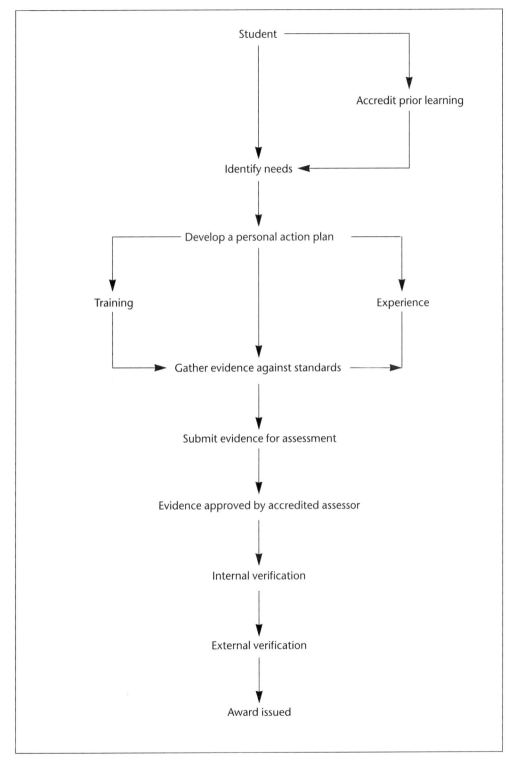

Figure 8.1: NVQ sport and recreation flowchart

The range of options available includes:

- Sport and recreation: Level 1.
- Sport and recreation in coaching and activity delivery for adults: Level 2.
- Sport and recreation in coaching adults: Level 3.
- Sport and recreation in coaching and activity delivery for children: Level 2.
- Sport and recreation in coaching children: Level 3.
- Sport and recreation in coaching those with disabilities: Level 3.
- Sport and recreation in development: Level 3.
- Sport and recreation in facility operations: Level 2.
- Sport and recreation in outdoor education: Level 3.
- Sport and recreation in supervision: Level 3.
- Sport and recreation in the management of facilities: Level 3.
- Sport and recreation in the management of sports development: Level 4.

The NVQ Sport and Recreation framework is progressive as each level builds up to form a competency-based qualification.

COMMUNITY LINKS

Physical Education Departments are at the forefront in developing positive links with local communities. Inmates competing in sporting events with local teams can learn valuable lessons in social behaviour, self-control, co-operation and respect for the rules. Developing these skills is as important as appreciating the need for sportsmanship and the concept of fair play.

Many PE departments share the sporting facilities in their establishment with outside groups. This allows some inmates to become involved with children and adult groups with special needs, such as those with physical disabilities and learning difficulties.

Community service projects are a feature of the regime in most establishments where Category D prisoners are located and in all Open Prisons. This involves work with local organisations, church groups, voluntary bodies and individuals with identifiable needs. Those who qualify for a facility licence have the opportunity to involve themselves in a wide range of projects, some of which generate positive publicity in the local media.

Some examples of the community service projects in an average establishment include:

- painting and decorating the flats of pensioners;
- gardening for those with learning difficulties;
- building wheelchair ramps for a day centre;
- refurbishing a church hall;
- repointing brickwork and rebuilding a church wall;
- assisting in the preparations for a summer fete at a hospice;
- erecting and dismantling the jumps at a horse show.

As part of the process of preparing for release, community service presents an opportunity for inmates to demonstrate they can be trusted and to develop their self-confidence and self-esteem.

SPENDING TIME IN THE OPEN AIR

Every inmate should be given the opportunity on a daily basis to spend time in the fresh air. This does not present a problem in open conditions or certain Category C prisons where the regime allows movement to work and activities outside on a daily basis.

The revised Prison Rule 27A and YOI Rule 38 no longer refers to the traditional entitlement of exercise. The current approach is that everyone should be able to choose how they spend their time in the fresh air, including sunbathing on a hot day as opposed to the traditional walk around an exercise yard.

Those in the segregation unit and unconvicted prisoners who have exercised their right not to work or attend the gymnasium are allowed one hour in the open air; everyone else should have 30 minutes. However, if the normal regime includes going outside the living accommodation to work or activity, then there is no obligation to make any additional arrangements.

If bad weather leads to the cancellation of time in the open air, association has to be offered as an alternative. When it is cold a donkey jacket should be available to use if a personal issue of a body-warmer or cagoule has not been made.

The revised Prison Rule 27 allows all adults the opportunity to attend the gym for one hour a week; Young Offenders are permitted two hours a week.

Anyone with special medical needs can attend remedial classes in the gym subject to the Medical Officer's approval. Everyone should be given the opportunity to take part in PE activities on weekdays, at the weekend or in evening classes.

THE EDUCATION SERVICE

The Education Service has an important part to play in the delivery of a positive regime within the establishment as its main aim is to address identified needs and help inmates to learn effectively. A variety of classes cater for a wide range of abilities. One priority is to help those with literacy and numeracy problems, including ethnic minorities for whom English is the second language. At the other end of the spectrum there are opportunities to study for a degree with the Open University, or undertake a wide range of academic courses which lead to nationally recognised qualifications.

Since 1993 the responsibility for providing the Education Service has been transferred from the Local Education Authority to an Educational Contractor, normally a college of further education awarded the contract by the Prison Department after submitting a competitive tender. The contract places an obligation on the successful contractor to provide a high-quality service based on the assessed needs of all inmates and offer them opportunities to gain accredited qualifications. The contracts are for an initial period of five years and during 1998 the competitive tendering process was repeated, with new contracts awarded from 1 January 1999.

One positive aspect of this arrangement is that the service provided is very flexible and is responsive to local changes in identified needs and preferences. Changes to the programme can be requested by an establishment, additional classes can be introduced and existing classes replaced in four weeks if necessary.

GAINING EDUCATIONAL QUALIFICATIONS

The education programme should be based on what is called a 'needs assessment' of each new reception's educational requirements.

A youngster under school-leaving age is obliged to attend a programme of compulsory education for a minimum of 15 hours a week. All other sentenced young offenders should be given the opportunity to take part in educational classes for at least 15 hours each week.

A comprehensive education programme should be available throughout the year. The National Operating Standard states that everyone should have the opportunity to attend classes on weekdays for 50 weeks of the year. Evening classes should be accessible on five nights a week for 42 weeks of the year.

The published programme should be flexible and cater for all needs irrespective of ethnic group and nationality. Some establishments recognise accredited educational achievements with qualification bonuses in addition to their normal earnings. Any qualifications obtained should result in the appropriate certificate being awarded.

Every establishment is expected to have gained the Basic Skill Quality Mark and provide a core curriculum which offers everyone the opportunity to acquire Basic Skills which include:

* helping everyone, including foreign inmates, to read, write and speak English clearly;
* carrying out simple mathematics at a level that allows inmates to cope adequately at work and in society generally;
* providing them with a basic understanding of the use of computers;
* social and life skills.

Since 1997 all subjects offered as part of the core curriculum should be accredited. Holding nationally recognised qualifications helps those wishing to continue their studies at a local college or enter the highly competitive job market.

The educational classes should offer the opportunity to gain the following qualifications:

* Wordpower and Numberpower at Entry Level; an acceptable alternative is Literacy and Numeracy which is offered by the Associated Examination Board (AEB).
* Wordpower and Numberpower at Level 1.
* Pitmans English for Speakers of Other Languages, ESOL, at Basic, Elementary and Intermediate levels.
* Wordpower and Numberpower at Level 2.
* GNVQ Foundation, Intermediate and Advanced.

- General Certificate of Secondary Education (GCSE).
- NVQ Levels 1, 2, and 3.
- Computer Literate Aided Information Technology (RSA CLAIT).
- RSA Firm Start Certificate.
- Health and Hygiene Basic, Intermediate and Advanced Certificates.
- Open College Levels 1, 2 and 3.
- Community Sports Leadership Award (CSLA).
- Access courses.
- Open University courses.
- Generic Preparation for Work course at Level 1, recognised by the Accreditation Syndicate for Education and Training (ASET).

ACQUIRING BASIC SKILLS

Research has shown that there is a serious basic skills deficiency in penal establishments which is significantly above the average for the population as a whole. If an inmate has literacy and numeracy difficulties it is worthwhile tackling this problem while in custody and improving the chances of obtaining work on release.

It is possible to gain basic skills while attending a vocational training course or while learning an industrial or practical skill. The biggest hurdle for most inmates is admitting they have a problem. Teachers have discovered many inmates are skilled at covering up their learning difficulties. In some instances their reticence is because they are concerned about the reaction of other inmates who discover they are non-functional readers.

The Basic Skills Agency (BSA) have defined basic skills as: 'the ability to read, write and speak in English and use mathematics at a level necessary to function and progress at work and in society in general'. They have established Quality Standards, which the Prison Service have adopted. The Education Contractor is expected to satisfy an external assessor that the standard of basic skills education provided includes the following:

- a confidential personal interview before tuition commences;
- a needs assessment using the Basic Skills Agency screening test;
- at least four hours of tuition each week;
- a low teacher–student ratio in classes;
- an agreed learning plan;
- a regular assessment of progress;
- the opportunity for accreditation of learning;
- quality of teaching that conforms to national standards;
- access to suitable learning material is available;
- racial differences and equal opportunity issues are respected.

Information Technology is another important part of the core curriculum. This involves gaining a basic understanding of computing including word processing, learning how to produce spreadsheets, computer graphics and the general skills of information gathering and retrieval.

The basic level of qualification offered is RSA CLAIT, but inmates can progress to Integrated Business Technology (IBT2). For those involved on a Vocational Training Course (VTC) there are opportunities to study for National Vocational Qualifications (NVQs).

An NVQ is a work-based qualification. The quality standard is decided by the organisations who represent employers and the professions. They identify the competencies, skill and performance levels necessary to actually do the job. The qualification framework is progressive which means students can acquire a number of single *units* in stages which collectively make up a *level*. These range from Level 1 (basic) up to Level 4 (advanced).

Education also provides the opportunity for all inmates to broaden their horizons and develop their potential by developing creative skills. Subjects such as Drama, Art, Pottery, Craft, Video Production and Music can spark an interest that can be life-changing. Many establishments offer an imaginative range of options and incorporate these into the local curriculum. Often creative skills are a significant part of the evening class programme.

SOCIAL AND LIFE SKILLS

The National Curriculum Framework of Core Skills is based on the recommendations of the report *The Future Direction of Education Provision in HM Prisons, Young Offender Institutions and Remand Centres* and was fully introduced into all establishments in 1997. It has four main programmes:

- Communications.
- Numeracy.
- Information Technology.
- Social and Life Skills.

The most recent addition is the Social and Life Skills programme which has been designed to complement other courses that address offending behaviour, such as the Sex Offender Treatment Programme, the Enhanced Thinking Skills Programme and the Reasoning and Rehabilitation Programme. Its purpose is to provide an opportunity to develop personal awareness, social, personal and vocational abilities. It aims to address inmates' needs and has proved valuable in developing their self-confidence and self-esteem.

After the induction interview and needs assessment have been completed by the Education Co-ordinator, inmates should be given an opportunity to attend this course, which can be incorporated into their sentence plan.

This course has been accredited, so for each module successfully completed *credits* are awarded which are equivalent to GCSE, NVQ and GNVQ. The Social and Life Skills curriculum is offered as an accredited course at three different levels:

1. *The Basic Skills Tests in Life Skills* accredited by the Associated Examination Board, which is suitable for YOIs.

2. *The Social and Life Skills Programme* accredited by the Open College Network, which is suitable for all penal establishments.
3. *The Diploma in Achievement* accredited by the Oxford and Cambridge Diploma in Achievement.

The Social and Life Skills Programme is offered at Level 1 and Level 2; each level comprises 11 units as follows:

1. Preparation for work.
2. Family relationships.
3. Parentcraft.
4. Working with others.
5. Budgeting and money management.
6. Cookery.
7. Do-it-yourself.
8. Healthy living.
9. Introduction to drug and alcohol awareness.
10. Improving assertiveness and decision-making.
11. Personal development.

Each unit of the programme requires 20 hours of teacher contact time to complete to the required standard.

The *Generic Preparation for Work* course was introduced in 1998 to supplement the Social and Life Skills programme. It has been developed to support the workshop expansion scheme, and while it targets industrial workshops, it is available to all inmates in every type of establishment. This course, accredited by ASET, offers one credit at Level 1 and requires 30 hours of teaching contact hours to complete.

RECORDS OF ACHIEVEMENT

The report *A National Framework for Prison Education,* produced in 1994, recommended that those attending education classes on a full- or part-time basis should have a record of their achievements maintained. In 1996 Young Offenders were included in the scheme for the first time. The *Record of Achievement* (ROA) in its present form is not yet suitable for adults and an appropriate version has yet to be devised by the Department for Education and Employment. In the meantime adult establishments are being encouraged to use a modified form of the current Record of Achievement.

The Record of Achievement is documentary evidence of educational and training experiences together with details of qualifications obtained. These details can be transferred to the receiving prison when a transfer takes place, thus maintaining continuity. The ROA provides evidence that an inmate has studied with the college that holds the education contract and makes no reference to the fact that the student has undertaken the course in custody.

The National Record of Achievement can be obtained in a burgundy coloured folder with plastic inserts to keep certificates and other evidence of prior learning intact. It is a nationally recognised portfolio which is accepted by prospective employers and colleges as a living document and also acts as an action plan for future development.

Further information and advice can be obtained by writing to: NCVQ, 222 Euston Road, London NW1 2BZ (for England, Wales and Northern Ireland); or SCOTVEC, Hanover House, 24 Douglas Street, Glasgow G2 7NQ (for Scotland).

COMPLETING VOCATIONAL TRAINING COURSES

One of the challenges facing inmates preparing for release is gaining suitable educational and vocational qualifications which will equip them to compete in the job market.

A wide range of Vocational and Construction Industry Training Courses is available throughout the country, leading to nationally recognised qualifications including NVQs. Inmates are informed during their period on induction if the following courses are available in their establishments:

- Beauty therapy.
- Braille.
- Bricklaying.
- Business studies.
- Computer-aided design.
- Computer graphics.
- Carpentry.
- Catering.
- Computing.
- Craft.
- Drawing office skills.
- Electrical installation.
- Electronic wiring.
- Fashion and design.
- Furniture craft.
- General construction.
- Hairdressing.
- Home economics.
- Home management.
- Horticulture.
- Industrial cleaning.
- Information technology.
- Light vehicle repairs.
- Machine setting.
- Mechanical engineering.
- Micro engineering.
- Model making.
- Motor cycle maintenance.
- Motor mechanics.
- Multi-skills.
- Occupational therapy.
- Office skills.
- Painting and decorating.
- Parentcraft.
- Plastering.
- Plumbing.
- Precision engineering.
- Radio/TV servicing.
- Skills training.
- Tailoring.
- Technical storekeeping.
- Tiling.
- Welding.

THE KOESTLER AWARD SCHEME

The purpose of the Koestler Award Scheme, whose Chairman is Sir Stephen Tumim, is to encourage and reward creative work produced by men, women and young people in penal establishments, secure units and special hospitals. It has been held annually since 1961. In 1998 a total of 4000 entries were received from establishments which covered 46 different categories of creative work. A successful entry can result in a cash prize of up to £100 and some of the sponsored awards are worth up to £500. All entries are returned to participating inmates unless they state that they wish their entry to be sold and the proceeds donated to the Prison Charity Shop Scheme.

A wide range of classes is available and entries are judged by experts in their own field. The main categories are as follows:

- Art.
- Sculpture, ceramics and craft.
- Woodcraft and soft furnishings.
- Soft toys.
- Needlecraft, needlepoint, knitting and crochet.
- Matchstich models.
- Prose and prison magazines.
- Poetry.
- Playwriting for stage.
- Playwriting for radio.
- Writing for television.
- Calligraphy and decorative calligraphy.
- Recycling.
- Music composition and lyrics.
- Computer skills.
- Vocational training courses: furniture, engineering and engineering designs.
- Dressmaking and tailoring.
- Prison enterprise services.
- Construction industry training.
- Physical education.
- Photography.
- Performance of the spoken word – poetry.
- Performance of the spoken word – drama.

Following judging the prizewinning entries are put on public display in a special exhibition held in the Atrium Gallery, Queensway, London, in September. The exhibition attracts in excess of 25,000 visitors.

Further information about the Koestler Exhibition and Trust can be obtained from the following address: The Koestler Award Trust, 9 Birchmead Avenue, Pinner, Middlesex HA5 2BG. Telephone: 0181–868 4044.

THE LIBRARY

Every establishment in co-operation with the local authority provides a library service. This allows inmates to exchange books, use the talking book service and gain access to information which helps with their educational, recreational and cultural needs. Books are available for those with learning disabilities, basic skills deficiencies, those whose first language is not English; the service also caters for the preferences of ethnic minorities.

The aim is to encourage inmates to develop a reading habit and learn how to make use of information, acquire a vocational skill, gain further educational qualifications and introduce them to the idea of reading for pleasure.

Inmates can seek advice from the professional librarian who regularly attends. He deals with special requests for books not in stock and supplies these from the public library. Many establishments have installed microfiche readers and computer terminals to allow inmates access to all books held by the library authority.

The prison library holds a book stock equivalent to 10 books per inmate, subject to there being a minimum book stock of 5000 volumes. In order to maintain variety and topicality new titles are periodically added, and a quarter of the titles should be exchanged annually.

Everybody should be allowed to visit the library for a minimum of 20 minutes each week, but if this is not possible for security reasons, arrangements should be made on the wing for library books to be changed.

The library is expected to include in the reference section a comprehensive range of publications, up-to-date editions of standard legal reference works and copies of relevant legislation. A full list of all the publications available in the library is listed in the Annex to Instruction to Governors 73/1996, which is available in the library on request. Publications available include:

- Acts and Guides to Acts; *The Prison Act 1952* published by The Stationery Office.
- Rules and Standing Orders; copies of all published sections of Standing Orders.
- Other Prison Service Guides and Manuals; *Foreign Prisoners' Resource Pack* produced by The Prison Reform Trust.
- Council of Europe and United Nations publications; *European Prison Rules* published by The Stationery Office.
- Reports and Enquiries; *The Report of the Parole Board* published by The Stationery Office.
- Legal Guidance; *Prisoners and the Law* by Creighton and King, and *Archbold's Criminal Pleading and Evidence* by Sweet and Maxwell.
- Other publications; *HM Chief Inspector of Prison Report* on the penal establishment where currently resident and *Vacher's Parliamentary Companion*.

DEVELOPING EMPLOYMENT SKILLS

The Prison Service runs manufacturing and assembly facilities in most establishments where a wide range of goods is produced by Regime Services. Opportunities thus exist to learn a trade and gain real work experience. Prison industries produce goods which are used in penal establishments throughout the country. There is also an increasing tendency for the Prison Service to develop partnership arrangements and operate workshops in conjunction with private firms, generating additional revenue.

Another initiative, the *Workshop Expansion Scheme,* identifies *Pathfinder* establishments which have efficiently run workshops which achieve agreed production targets and cater for the internal market. The objective is to support them achieving comparable production to outside industries by the introduction of a normal working day.

Those employed can receive enhanced wages by way of recognising their contribution to productivity and gain valuable work experience. Under the enhanced earnings scheme participants can earn up to three times the average earnings paid to other inmates.

The range of work currently available (and discussed below) throughout the whole of Regime Services is as follows:

- Agriculture.
- Brush manufacture.
- Clothing, textiles and weaving.
- Concreting.
- Contract services.
- Engineering.
- Footwear and leather goods.
- Laundry.
- Plastics.
- Printing.
- Woodworking.

Over the past few years prison industries have received a considerable amount of investment which has transformed traditional workshops in some establishments into modern industrial units. In new prisons modern manufacturing and assembly facilities have been installed.

The aim of prison industries is to provide high-quality products and offer meaningful work in the form of industrial training. This is mutually beneficial as it helps inmates gain skills that will increase the likelihood of gaining work on release and allows the Prison Service to develop partnerships with the private sector which bring in additional revenue. It also allows those on the enhanced wages scheme to save money for their release.

PRISON INDUSTRIES

Agriculture

A quarter of the food consumed in prisons and Young Offender Institutions is produced by 2500 inmates employed on the 31 farms owned by the Prison Service.

There they can learn animal husbandry skills as they care for the cows, pigs, chickens and rare breeds which are raised on a commercial basis. There is scope to develop knowledge about milk production (20 million pints are produced each year) and packaging for distribution to different establishments.

Horticulture skills can be developed in the farms and gardens that cultivate a full range of ornamental plants in addition to a wide range of vegetable produce. Work in farms and gardens is practically based and lends itself to the National Vocational Qualification (NVQ) system of gaining work-based qualifications.

Brush manufacture

There is only one workshop in the country. This produces a selection of paint and cleaning brushes, and manufactures brooms using hand-fill pitch and tar machine-filled processes.

Clothing, textiles and weaving

This is the largest manufacturing group and employs 4300 inmates in 83 workshops. They are involved in producing a wide range of protective clothing, overalls, kitchen whites, donkey jackets, duffle coats, denim jackets and trousers. Underwear, a range of shirts and casual wear is produced including PE shorts, tracksuits and pyjamas; bed linen, blankets, mattress covers, towels and socks are all made in-house.

Inmates can learn about textiles, tailoring, shirt-making, weaving, knitting, inter-locking, sewing and general cutting processes.

Concreting

Two workshops employ 50 inmates making slabs, posts and a selection of building blocks and panels. They can learn about handfill moulding and vibrated machine moulding.

Contract services

Nationally there are 71 workshops employing 1500 inmates in a range of services, including electrical and component assembly work, testing printed circuit boards, packing, shrink wrapping and data processing. Even the training dummies used by the fire and ambulance services are produced in contract service workshops.

Engineering

Seventeen workshops employ a further 700 making lockers, shelving, chairs, beds, information signs, windows, doors, catering equipment together with a range of security products to keep the prison population safely inside. All the security gates, grilles and windows are manufactured in-house.

The processes involved include sheet-metal pressing, powder coating, welding, sign-making, tube manipulation, turning, milling, drilling, punching and work with stainless steel and aluminium.

Footwear and leather goods

Five workshops, including one specialising in leather goods and industrial gloves, employ 170 inmates who produce safety boots and shoes, sports shoes, trainers and slippers. They can learn string lasting and slipper-making processes.

Laundry

There are 42 laundries throughout the country which employ 900 inmates. The work includes laundering sheets, pillow cases, blankets, duvets, shirts, trousers, tableclothes, towels, aprons, jackets, coats and boiler suits.

Plastics

There are four injection-moulding workshops and three vacuum-forming workshops which employ 70. They manufacture small components, plastic and polymer subcontract mouldings. Flower and seedling trays, boxes, containers and packaging products are also produced. The processes involved are injection moulding and vacuum forming.

Printing

The 11 printing workshops employ 190 inmates who print brochures, product support literature and manuals. A bookbinding and restoration service is available and graphic design, 3D modelling, animation services, electronic printing and litho printing are undertaken to a high standard.

Woodworking

There are 17 workshops across the country providing employment for 700. They produce a wide range of goods including sheds, pallets, furniture, chairs, tables, loudspeaker cabinets, windows, doors and specialised joinery products. The processes include sawing, planing, shaping, moulding, jointing, sanding, assembling, upholstering, painting and staining.

Of the 130 penal establishments in England and Wales, 46 have achieved the quality standard ISO 9002, formerly British Standards (BS 5750).

WORK EXPERIENCE

The aim is to provide sufficient work places to allow everyone to carry out purposeful work based on a normal working day. In addition to working in prison industries, attending education classes or vocational and construction industry training, most establishments have several other work parties providing useful work.

- *Domestic cleaning* takes place on each wing where several inmates are employed under the supervision of prison officers. The job is to keep the wing clean and tidy, clear away rubbish and help serve food at meal times. In some establishments qualifications in Industrial Cleaning can be obtained.
- *The Kitchen Party* is one of the most popular and highly paid work parties. Those with previous experience of cooking, baking, vegetable preparation and general catering experience are likely to be in demand. It is necessary to gain the Basic Hygiene Certificate, but there are opportunities in many establishments to obtain NVQs in Catering.
- *The Works Department* are responsible for general maintenance and repairs to the fabric of the establishment. They employ those with an existing trade as well as providing work experience for those who successfully complete a Construction Industry Training course.
- *The Gardens Party,* popular in the summer, provides opportunities to keep all the gardens and grounds neat and tidy.

- *Orderlies* and *'red-bands'* occupy jobs which involve a degree of trust. 'Red-bands' tend to be unsupervised and have freedom of movement around the establishment, once they have been vetted by the Security Department who issue identification cards and a red band which is worn on the arm. 'Red-bands' work in areas like the Officers' Mess, Reception and the Hospital. Orderlies are employed on the wings to collect and serve the food, operate the wing laundries, work in the Stores and in the Gate Lodge.
- *The Grounds Party* empty the bins, pick up litter and take rubbish on a daily basis to the skips.

Pay rates reflect productivity, the skill level and degree of trust attached to the job. Some work, such as work in the kitchen or as 'red-bands', is restricted to those on the enhanced regime.

CASE STUDIES

Rudd Basho gains basic educational skills

Rudd Basho is 17 years old and serving his first sentence of Youth Custody. He left school without gaining any educational qualifications and was unable to find a job. On Induction he is seen by the Education Department who carry out a needs assessment and discover he underachieves because he is illiterate. He is accepted for full-time education and his classes concentrate on the core curriculum. His timetable includes Wordpower and Numberpower at entry level to help him with his reading and writing difficulties, and he is introduced to computers which he enjoys and which encourage him to learn to spell. Rudd also attends Social and Life Skills classes where he learns about preparing for work, budgeting and how to improve his assertiveness and decision-making ability. One evening a week he voluntarily attends a class on making soft toys, as he has recently become a father.

Peter Miles develops his physical fitness in the gymnasium

Peter Miles is a regular offender in his early thirties and is interested in keeping fit. The Medical Officer assesses him on reception as Fit 1A which means he is able to take part in the full range of activities in the gymnasium. He becomes interested in weight-lifting and is encouraged to develop his potential by gaining the Community Sports Leadership Award (CSLA). Peter gains the basic CSLA qualification and decides to try and obtain work on release in the leisure industry. With this in mind he embarks on a course of study, aiming to qualify with an NVQ in Sports and Recreation, coaching adults.

Paddy Naughtie learns an employment skill

Paddy Naughtie is a professional criminal who received a life sentence for the murder of a night watchman while committing an armed robbery. He has tended to avoid hard work, preferring an easy but aimless life in prison. All attempts to interest him in learning an employment skill have been unsuccessful, but since he has developed a serious relationship with his penfriend, Paddy now feels he has a future. He decides it is time to acquire a skill and applies to join the Welding VTC course. The Security Department are wary about his motives, but Paddy is allowed to attend and successfully completes the course. Regime Services have an Engineering Workshop in the establishment making lockers, security gates and grilles, and the Industrial Manager is keen to utilise his skills. Paddy proves to be a skilled welder, and receives excellent wages in recognition of his productivity and the quality of his work.

Nicola Harrington enters the Koestler Award Scheme

Nicola Harrington has finally settled into prison life after a difficult start. She develops a talent for needlecraft while attending evening classes run by the Education Department, and makes some beautiful dresses for her baby born in custody. Her teacher is impressed with the quality of her work and persuades her to enter the Koestler Award Scheme. Whilst her entry does not win a prize, it is accepted for public display in the exhibition which is held annually in London.

CHECKLIST

- How are inmates classified fit for Physical Education?
- Describe the operation of the employment classification system.
- What is the role of the Basic Skills Agency?
- Which vocational and construction industry training courses are provided?
- What work experience does Prison Service Enterprises provide?

- What is the weekly entitlement to physical education?
- How has the traditional entitlement to exercise changed as a result of the revised Prison Rule 27A?
- Describe the four components of the core curriculum.
- How are National Vocational Qualifications obtained?
- Is the prison library obliged to keep standard legal reference books and copies of legislation available for consultation?

- What qualifications are necessary to obtain work as an instructor in Physical Education?
- How can a 'record of achievement' assist inmates after release?
- Outline the purpose of the Koestler Award Scheme.
- Which prison industries provide most employment for inmates?
- Who qualifies for enhanced wages?

DISCUSSION POINTS

1. 'All prisoners identified as having a recognised mental illness should be transferred to an outside hospital.' Discuss.

2. Examine the extent to which the risks associated with taking part in contact sports outweigh the benefits.

3. Consider how appropriate it is to release prisoners on facility licence to take part in community service projects when the courts can make a Community Service Order as an alternative to custody.

4. The revised Prison Rule 27A has replaced the requirement to provide exercise with an entitlement to time in the open air. What difference does this make?

5. Should all prisoners identified on Induction with a basic skills deficiency be obliged to attend educational classes?

6. Discuss whether all work and training experiences should be accredited, thus equipping everyone to compete effectively in the job market on release.

CHAPTER 9

Making Resettlement Plans

THROUGHCARE

The Criminal Justice Act 1991 introduced the radical idea of Throughcare into sentencing policy, where those convicted serve part of their sentence in prison and the balance in the community under statutory supervision. Throughcare applies to anyone sent to prison or a Young Offender Institution for 12 months or more.

The process begins following sentencing and includes the following:

- conducting a thorough needs assessment;
- developing a sentence plan;
- carrying out a risk assessment;
- confronting offending behaviour;
- helping inmates to resettle successfully on release;
- supervision on release until the period on licence has been completed.

An unconvicted prisoner or Young Offender will be presumed to be innocent of any charges they are facing. The only reason to hold them in custody is to ensure they can be physically produced in court when the court requires them to appear.

The principles of Throughcare still apply but the emphasis is on:

- offering advice and help with any personal or family difficulties, financial problems, health care concerns including any addiction to drugs or alcohol;
- allowing them the opportunity to apply for bail or meet any bail conditions imposed by the court. This may include helping to find suitable accommodation if they are applying for bail but have nowhere to live;
- advising how to keep an existing job and home;
- assisting to keep in contact with family and friends.

A joint approach

The Prison Service and Probation Service published *The National Framework for the Throughcare of Offenders* in 1993, setting out the policy of both services with the intention of working to help inmates prepare effectively for their return to the community on discharge. Each establishment should have a Throughcare Policy Group with responsibility to manage and co-ordinate the delivery of the core elements of through-care.

Although probation officers and personal prison officers are there to be supportive the onus is on the individuals once convicted and sentenced to channel their efforts towards addressing any problems and preparing for their eventual release. This involves:

- accepting responsibility for their offending behaviour, considering the consequences of their actions on the victim;
- identifying ways to reduce the likelihood of re-offending;
- coming to terms with the sentence imposed;
- facing up to any personal problems;
- keeping in contact with family and friends;
- preparing a release plan.

In order to achieve these objectives, certain issues need to be identified and addressed in custody if the cycle of offending is to be broken. The following questions can be used as a checklist:

- Is there a problem with drugs and alcohol?
- Can they budget sensibly and provide adequately for their family?
- Do they have a problem keeping a job?
- Are they facing housing problems?
- Do they have a problem with literacy and numeracy?
- Do they lack self-confidence?
- Have they acquired sufficient employment training skills and work experience to be able to find work?
- Do they know how to be a good parent?
- Can they get on with their family without conflict and constant rows?
- Are they suffering racial discrimination?
- Are there any other obstacles they are facing which are preventing them from resolving any of these problems?

ADDRESSING OFFENDING BEHAVIOUR

Groupwork is a tried and tested approach which helps to address offending behaviour, as it allows learning to take place in a supportive setting alongside others facing similar problems.

Some of the learning techniques, like role-play, can only be used in a group setting. Role-play allows individuals to rehearse their likely response in a given situation making use of video equipment and feedback from other members of the group.

An effective groupwork programme needs to:

- have a *cognitive-behavioural approach* which tries to change the way individuals react by helping them to appreciate the connection between the way they think and the way they behave;

- be *firmly structured*;
- be *multi-modal*, tackling the whole range of problems they are facing at the same time;
- be based on a *conceptual model* with a sound theoretical understanding of the behaviour it is trying to change;
- be *needs-based* and demonstrate an appreciation of the individual's needs;
- be *responsivity-orientated*, using techniques like role-play and modelling which are known to be effective;
- have *clearly defined targets*;
- involve *outside agencies*;
- avoid *eroding conditions* like returning those who complete a drug treatment programme to a wing which contains drug users;
- provide *support* to the group leaders;
- be regularly reviewed and *independently evaluated* to make certain the agreed aims and objectives are being achieved.

THE SEX OFFENDER TREATMENT PROGRAMME

A number of establishments, including Young Offender Institutions, are running *Sex Offender Treatment Programmes* (SOTP), which are cognitive-behavioural programmes based on practice that has proved successful in other countries. They use a number of treatment methods which include brainstorming, discussion, role-play and arousal modification techniques.

There are five identifiable stages in the treatment process:

1. *Assessment* through individual interviews, psychological questionnaires and a penile plethysmograph, which assesses their response to sexual arousal.
2. *The Core Programme* consists of 70 × two-hour sessions which aim to:
   - encourage them to accept responsibility for their behaviour;
   - develop empathy with the suffering they have caused to the victim;
   - understand what causes them to commit offences;
   - identify the circumstances likely to increase the prospect of re-offending;
   - assist them to learn coping strategies to resist temptation.
3. *Cognitive Skills Training* addresses the thinking and reasoning processes which result in impulsive behaviour or in having difficulty resolving conflict. The two programmes currently in use are:
   - The *Reasoning and Rehabilitation Programme* which was imported from the Canadian Correctional Service. Its syllabus includes values enhancement, problem-solving skills, creative thinking, critical thinking, interpersonal skills and managing the emotional side of life.
   - The *Thinking Skills Programme* covers impulse control, rigid thinking, creative thinking, problem-solving, perspective-taking and decision-making.
4. *Deviant Arousal Modification* modules aim to help those at greatest risk of re-offending who are aroused by sexual violence and children.
5. *The Relapse Prevention Programme* is a booster or refresher programme which provides a further opportunity for individuals to enhance their coping strategies. It

presumes they are never completely cured and concentrates on *relapse prevention* in the final 12 months before release.

PRE-RELEASE COURSES

Inmate Development and Pre-Release Courses have been designed to help inmates to cope with imprisonment and enable them successfully to resettle back into the community on release. These courses aim to build confidence and self-esteem, modify a poor attitude, encourage individuals to realize their potential, learn new skills and heighten sensitivity towards others. In addition they provide practical advice about finding work, seeking accommodation, claiming benefits and health-care matters.

There are eleven modules in the complete course:

1. The *communications* package helps improve communication skills and encourages a greater awareness of the needs of others.
2. The *relationship* package promotes self-awareness and assists individuals to tackle relationship difficulties.
3. The *problem drinking* package increases knowledge about the negative effects of alcohol.
4. The *drugs* package increases awareness about the risks associated with illicit drug-taking.
5. The *gambling* package examines the risks and problems gambling can cause.
6. The *accommodation* package assists individuals to develop strategies for finding suitable accommodation.
7. The *money matters* package helps them budget effectively and avoid the dangers of getting into debt.
8. The *standing up for your rights* package explains how to exercise their consumer and civil rights.
9. The *practical information* package imparts information about home maintenance, energy conservation, environmental issues, health-care matters, survival cooking and using public transport.
10. The *work subject* package focuses on providing information and advice which will help inmates re-enter the world of work.
11. The *time on your hands* package encourages the wise use of leisure time and examines ways of tackling problems facing the unemployed.

The multi-disciplinary nature of the Inmate Development and Pre-Release Course means prison officers, teachers, probation officers, psychologists, chaplains, PE instructors and health care staff can all be involved in delivering parts of the programme. The course is in modular form, so those parts relevant to any identified needs can be incorporated into the sentence plan at the Induction stage.

All these courses complement the Throughcare approach introduced in the Criminal Justice Act 1991 and provide the opportunity to learn a range of skills which are useful in custody and designed to reduce the likelihood of re-offending.

PRE-RELEASE EMPLOYMENT SCHEMES (PRES)

There are seven hostels around the country which are adjacent to prisons holding long-term prisoners. This allows some inmates the opportunity to spend the last six months of their sentence living and working in the community before final discharge. While still subject to prison discipline while living in a PRES hostel the opportunity is valuable as it allows them to prepare for release by obtaining training and work experience, saving money from their earnings and obtaining a permanent job on release.

Some establishments run job clubs where advice and guidance is available to help inmates conduct a job search, prepare a curriculum vitae (CV), handle the disclosure of convictions to a prospective employer and develop interview skills. This can lead to their making applications for jobs, attending interviews on a facility licence, and if they receive job offers, taking part in a working-out scheme. Under this scheme they work normally during the day at their place of employment but return to the establishment each night. Inmates are eligible to take part in this initiative if they qualify for the enhanced regime and a risk assessment has been completed.

Training and Enterprise Councils (TECs) have a responsibility for employment training and youth training schemes throughout the country. They can assist with any employment training needs before and after release as they co-ordinate training in the area and have close links with employers and colleges of further education in the locality.

SUPERVISION IN THE COMMUNITY

On release the positive steps taken to reduce the likelihood of re-offending should continue in the community under the supervision of the outside probation officer, who is responsible for checking compliance with the licence conditions.

Approximately eight weeks before release a pre-discharge report is sent to the outside probation officer. This advises when the inmate is being discharged, how long he will be on supervision and any other relevant information that may be helpful to them in preparing the release plan.

About two weeks prior to release the personal prison officer should complete and send to the outside probation officer a discharge report, which will briefly outline how the inmate has used his time in custody.

Once a period of imprisonment is over, inmates can complete the remainder of their sentence in the community under the supervision of the Probation Service. This will last, for those serving over 12 months, until three-quarters of the sentence is reached.

The supervising probation officer has a statutory responsibility to supervise those discharged while on licence. Their main aims are:

- to protect the public, particularly where there has been a conviction involving an offence against children;
- to prevent further re-offending;
- to help them adjust from being an inmate in custody to being a parent with family responsibilities.

Although the Probation Service has a care and control role in relation to its clients while on licence, the supervising probation officer will wish to prevent difficulties arising on release. After release the individual under supervision should contact his probation officer immediately the first signs of any difficulties arise, and not wait until they have committed further offences.

The Probation Service has made it very clear that it takes seriously its responsibilities to help inmates on discharge. To demonstrate its commitment it has published a Statement of Purpose (see Preface, p. vii).

Schedule One offenders

Schedule One of the Children and Young Persons Act 1933 lists all the offences covered by these arrangements which includes all forms of child abuse, sexual assault, neglect, incest, infanticide, manslaughter and murder.

Once an individual has been identified as a Schedule One offender the local authority Social Services Department and the Probation Service are kept informed of his movements including any periods of temporary release that are approved. This is fully explained to inmates, who receive a formal notification which they are required to acknowledge. Close liaison between the Social Services and Probation departments takes place to make sure arrangements for their aftercare and supervision are in place prior to release.

The Probation Service may feel it appropriate to recommend to the Governor additional licence conditions in the case of anyone subject to automatic conditional release. Inmates who are granted discretionary conditional release or release on life licence may be subject to additional licence conditions at the direction of the Parole Board.

An example of a licence issued to inmates released under the Criminal Justice Act 1991 can be seen on p. 177. Any additional conditions that are included for child protection reasons will conform to the National Standards for the Supervision of Offenders in the Community.

Sex offenders

The Sex Offenders Act 1997 requires inmates serving a prison sentence for certain sexual offences to inform the police of their whereabouts on release. Schedule 1 of the Act lists fully all the offences covered by these arrangements; they include those convicted of rape, intercourse with a girl under 15, incest by a man, buggery, indecent asault and anyone acting as a pimp.

On release, inmates subject to this legislation are formally advised that they are required to notify the police of their discharge address and any subsequent change of address, and they are given a formal notification which they are required to acknowledge. See p. 176 for an example of this form.

The requirement for sex offenders to register their particulars with the police, known as the *registration period*, depends on the length of sentence they received. The period that applies for offenders under the age of 18 on the date of conviction is half the time applicable to adults. Table 9.1 gives details of registration periods.

Table 9.1: Registration periods

Sentence	Registration period	
	Over 18 on conviction	Under 18 on conviction
Over 30 months including life	Indefinite	Indefinite
Anyone subject to a hospital restriction order	Indefinite	Indefinite
More than six months but less than 30 months	10 years	5 years
Six months or less	7 years	3½ years
Anyone admitted to hospital but not subject to a restriction order	7 years	3½ years
A person of any other description	5 years	2½ years

PREPARING FOR RELEASE

When the time comes for release inmates are provided with:

- a travel warrant to take them home, either by bus or on the train, irrespective of whether they qualify for a discharge grant;
- all their private cash and any outstanding earnings due since last paid;
- any certificates and qualifications gained while in prison;
- all their personal possessions and any items of stored property being kept in reception;
- a standard discharge grant or a homeless rate discharge grant;
- a copy and explanation of the terms of any period of statutory supervision and if applicable the details of the parole licence.

All the licence conditions should be carefully explained before discharge. This includes discussing the period of supervision and the likely consequences of ignoring any of the conditions. A breach of any of the conditions of licence can result in being brought back to court and being fined up to £400 or given a further sentence of up to 30 days.

The licence states clearly the reporting instructions and where the supervising probation officer can be contacted. It also makes it clear that inmates remain *at risk* in the community until the sentence expiry date (SED) is reached.

Discharge grant

An application for a discharge grant can be made six weeks before the date of release. A discharge grant is only payable if the criteria laid down are met, as it is intended to replace that which would otherwise be received from the Benefits Agency during the first week back in the community.

Inmates do not receive a discharge grant if they are:

- under 16 years of age;
- serving a period of imprisonment of less than 14 days;
- a fine defaulter;
- in custody for non-payment of Council Tax;
- a civil prisoner;
- being held on remand;
- awaiting deportation;
- being held in a police cell;
- being transferred immediately to hospital;
- travelling to an address outside the UK;
- not eligible to receive Income Support.

The type of Discharge Grant depends on age and where the inmate plans to live on release. No one under the age of 18 is given a discharge grant unless there is an urgent need to pay for prearranged accommodation before release.

Most inmates who intend to return home to their family or their own accommodation will receive a *standard discharge grant* which is equivalent to one week's Income Support.

If they cannot return home and are likely to be homeless despite every effort made to find them suitable accommodation, the larger *homeless rate discharge grant* is paid. This grant covers the additional costs involved in providing accommodation in a hostel, in lodgings or in Bed and Breakfast.

CLAIMING ENTITLEMENTS

The Benefits Agency have produced a booklet in collaboration with NACRO, the Prison Service and several voluntary agencies entitled *Prisoners and their Families – A Guide to Benefits* which is obtainable within establishments on request.

On release most inmates qualify for help from the Benefits Agency. Their first priority is to sign on as soon as possible after discharge and qualify for Income Support. Benefit is payable fortnightly in arrears; this can cause difficulties if no funds apart from the discharge grant are available until their claim has been processed. If help is needed in the intervening period a *Crisis Loan* may be the only solution; but this has to be repaid eventually in the ensuing weeks.

- *Income Support* can be claimed provided a claimant is over the age of 16 and income is below a certain level. It is paid irrespective of availability for work and discharged inmates qualify for help if they are sick, disabled, heavily pregnant, a single parent, over retirement age, or in receipt of Invalid Care Allowance. Provided their assets are less than £8,000 and they are not working more than 16 hours a week, they qualify for assistance.
  Leaflet IS1 *Income Support* or IS20 *A Guide to Income Support* can be obtained from the local Benefits Agency.
- A *Jobseeker's Allowance* can be claimed by anyone available to work or actively

seeking and capable of work. The rate depends on personal circumstances, age, and whether it is a contribution-based or income-based application.

Leaflet JSAL5 *Jobseeker's Allowance* should be consulted for further details.

- *Crisis Loans* are available to anyone facing a genuine emergency and unable to meet their short-term expenses.
- Applications for *Housing Benefit* and *Council Tax Benefit* can be made to the Council if help is needed in paying the rent and Council Tax.

Help towards mortgage interest payments, some service charges and heating costs is not available. Nor can applications be made if claimants have more than £16,000 in savings. Any rent allowance approved depends on personal circumstances and is also restricted to the average cost of a single self-contained room in the area.

Leaflet RR1 *Housing Benefit – Help with your Rent* and RR2 *A Guide to Housing Benefit and Council Tax Benefit* can be obtained from either the Council or the local Benefits Agency.

- A *Community Care Grant* can be claimed if help is needed re-establishing inmates in the community. Anyone intending to claim Income Support on release with special needs can make an application for a Community Grant up to six weeks before their discharge. The supervising probation officer or local Citizens Advice Bureau may be able to offer help in making a claim. The inmate's family can claim Income Support when they return home temporarily on resettlement leave provided they are already in receipt of Income Support or the Jobseeker's Allowance.

Further details are contained in leaflet SF300 available from the local Benefits Agency.

- Anyone responsible for caring for a severely disabled person may qualify for an *Invalid Care Allowance* provided they already qualify for the middle or highest rate of *Disability Living Allowance.*

Further details are contained in leaflet SD4 *Caring for Someone?* and the claim pack DS700 available from the local Benefits Agency.

OTHER BENEFITS

Other practical help may be available from the local Benefits Agency office, depending on individual circumstances.

- *Family credit*
  Obtain leaflet NI261 *A Guide to Family Credit.*
- *Help with health costs*
  Obtain leaflet HC11 *Are you entitled to help with health costs?*
- *Cold weather payments*
  Obtain leaflet CWP1 *Extra help with heating costs when it's very cold.*
- *Child support maintenance*
  Obtain leaflet CSA 2001 *For Parents who live apart.*
- *Statutory sick pay*
  Obtain leaflet N1244SSP *Check your Rights.*

The Benefits Agency produce more than 100 leaflets which explain the range of assistance available. They have expanded their website on the Internet to over 1000 pages and it is regularly updated. The website can be found at *http://www.dss.gov.uk.*

WELFARE TO WORK PROGRAMMES

In 1998, as part of the Government's *Welfare to Work* programme a New Deal for young unemployed persons was introduced. It is designed to help those aged 18–24 who have been unemployed for over six months.

Pilot programmes lasting eight weeks are being introduced into 11 establishments. These intensive job-skill programmes are targeted at Young Offenders with the aim of helping them to acquire educational and job-hunting skills and gain employment on release.

The Benefits Agency have set up a New Deal Information Line on 0845–606 2626, and have a New Deal website at www.newdeal.gov.uk.

HELPLINES

The Benefits Agency produce a useful booklet, MG1 *A Guide to Benefits,* which is a concise guide to benefits and pensions. Further advice can be obtained from the local Benefits Agency office.

A number of Helplines can also be contacted for advice. The 0800 numbers are free of charge and the 0345 numbers are charged at local rates.

* Benefit Enquiry Line   0800–88 22 00
* Child Support Agency National Enquiry Line 0345–133 133
* Disability Living Allowance Helpline   0345–123 456
* Family Credit Helpline   01253–50 00 50
* Health Information Line   0800–65 55 44
* Pensions Info-Line   0345–31 32 33
* Fuel Payments Helpline   0645–15 15 15

Many of the guides and leaflets are available in large print, as audio tapes or in Braille, for those with special needs. They also provide material for ethnic minorities in the following languages.

* Bengali.
* Chinese.
* Greek.
* Gujarati.
* Hindi.
* Polish.
* Punjabi.
* Somali.
* Sylheti.

- Turkish.
- Urdu.
- Vietnamese.
- Welsh.

THE REHABILITATION OF OFFENDERS ACT 1974

An ex-offender is under a legal obligation to tell a prospective employer about any convictions he has if asked, unless they are *spent*.

The Rehabilitation of Offenders Act 1974 allows offenders legally to forget a criminal conviction after a *rehabilitation period*. This helps to counter prejudice against ex-offenders which can nullify all their efforts to make a fresh start.

The length of the rehabilitative period directly relates to the length of sentence and not the time actually spent in custody. In the case of a sentence of 2½ years or more it never becomes *spent*.

There are a number of exceptions to the Rehabilitation of Offenders Act where previous convictions must be disclosed.

- Applications to join certain professions where legal protection applies, including accountants, chemists, dentists, doctors, lawyers and nurses.
- Appointments to certain sensitive occupations which give access to children and youngsters under the age of 18. This includes childminders, foster parents, prison officers, the police, probation officers, school caretakers, social workers, teachers, traffic wardens and youth workers.
- Certain regulated occupations, including casino operators, directors and managers of insurance companies and unit trusts, firearms dealers and nursing home proprietors.
- Appointments to jobs where national security could be compromised, including certain posts in the civil service and defence contractors.
- Applications for firearm certificates, shotguns or explosives.

When applying for a job ex-offenders are entitled to answer *'No'* to any question on the application form or at interview that refers to a spent conviction, provided the job in question is not exempt from the Act. An untruthful answer to a question that refers to *unspent* convictions can lead to possible prosecution. Obtaining a job by deceiving an employer is also grounds for instant dismissal.

The period of rehabilitation that applies under the Act depends on how old the offender is on conviction. If he was convicted under the age of 17, a shorter period of rehabilitation is applicable, as Table 9.2 (page 138) illustrates.

Agencies such as the APEX TRUST offer help, advice and guidance with employment problems. They publish literature encouraging employers to pursue equal opportunity policies and not discriminate against ex-offenders. They have offices throughout the country but can be contacted through their Headquarters: APEX TRUST, St Alphage House, Wingate Annex, 2 Fore Street, London EC2Y 5DA. Telephone: 0171–638 5931.

REPATRIATION

A foreign national convicted and sentenced to a term of imprisonment can under certain circumstances return to his own country to serve a prison sentence. The same right applies to British nationals who are included in the international agreement under The Repatriatation of Prisoners Act 1984. This legislation allows sentenced prisoners from member countries who are not appellants, to be considered.

Applications for repatriation can be considered by citizens of the following 28 countries covered by the agreement.

- Austria.
- Bahamas.
- Belgium.
- Bulgaria.
- Canada.
- Croatia.
- Cyprus.
- Czech Republic.
- Denmark.
- Finland.
- France.
- Germany.
- Greece.
- Hungary.
- Iceland.
- Ireland.
- Italy.
- Luxembourg.
- Malta.
- Netherlands.
- Norway.
- Poland.
- Spain.
- Sweden.
- Switzerland.
- Trinidad and Tobago.
- Turkey.
- United States of America.

Table 9.2: Rehabilitation periods

SENTENCE	REHABILITATION PERIOD	
	Over 17 on conviction	*Under 17 on conviction*
PRISON or YOUTH CUSTODY of more than 6 months and less than 2½ years	10 years	5 years
PRISON or YOUTH CUSTODY of less than 6 months	7 years	3½ years
FINE or COMMUNITY SERVICE ORDER	5 years	2½ years
ABSOLUTE DISCHARGE	6 months	3 months
PROBATION, SUPERVISION, CARE ORDER, CONDITIONAL DISCHARGE or BIND-OVER	1 year or until the order expires, whichever is the longer	
ATTENDANCE CENTRE ORDER	1 year after the order expires	
HOSPITAL ORDERS with or without a restriction order	5 years or 2 years after the order expires, whichever is the longer.	

A Commonwealth Repatriation Scheme covers the following five countries:

- Canada.
- Malawi.
- Nigeria.

- Trinidad and Tobago.
- Zimbabwe.

A bilateral agreement exists between Great Britain and Thailand.
Members of the following dependent territories can apply for repatriation:

- Anguilla.
- British Indian Ocean Territory.
- British Virgin Islands.
- Cayman Islands.
- Falkland Islands.

- Gibraltar.
- Montserrat.
- Pitcairn Islands.
- Sovereign Base Area Cyprus.
- St Helena and dependencies.

Inmates covered by one of these existing agreements can apply using the Request and Complaints procedure, or through their consular officials. Requests are handled at Prison Service Headquarters, but they take a minimum of six months to process depending on the country involved.

Consideration for a request for repatriation will only be considered if the following criteria are satisfied:

- the inmate is a citizen of one of the countries listed above;
- there is no appeal outstanding;
- at least six months of the sentence remains;
- the offence committed would have led to a custodial sentence in the inmate's own country;
- both countries involved agree to the request;
- the inmate gives formal consent.

Anyone wishing to apply for a transfer to Scotland, Northern Ireland, the Channel Islands or the Isle of Man must satisfy the following conditions unless there are strong compassionate or other exceptional reasons:

- at least six months left to serve;
- normally resident in that country prior to sentence;
- close family living there and there is intention to reside there on release;
- he would be able to receive family visits;
- he does not present a high security risk, and is not a disruptive or subversive prisoner.

An application for repatriation or transfer is likely to be approved if the offence is not very serious and the sentence would not be significantly reduced as a consequence of repatriation.

CASE STUDIES

Rudd Basho prepares for release under supervision

Rudd Basho is coming to the end of his first custodial sentence of 12 months and is being released on his Conditional Release Date. The conditions of his supervision licence are explained to him and he appreciates he will be under the supervision of a probation officer for three months until his Sentence Expiry Date. He has been advised that he is subject to the Rehabilitation of Offenders Act for five years, as he was convicted when he was under 17 years old. During Rudd's final weeks he attended a Pre-release course and now plans to obtain a flat to live with Lola, his girlfriend, and their baby, who currently reside in a hostel. In the interim he plans to return to his parents and has made enquiries about how to claim Income Support and Housing Benefit. He qualifies for a Standard Discharge Grant which he receives together with his property, private cash, earnings for the previous week and a travel warrant home.

Peter Miles addresses his offending behaviour

Peter Miles is serving his fourth custodial sentence of five years imprisonment for illegally importing drugs and supplying them to young people. His pattern of offending shows he has a dependency problem, with alcohol featuring largely in earlier offending. Peter was eligible to be considered for parole at the halfway stage of his sentence but his application was declined. He decides to apply for a place on an Inmate Development and Pre-Release course and successfully completes three modules: Drugs, Problem Drinking and Relationships. Peter is released on supervision on reaching his Non Parole Date having served two-thirds or 3 years 4 months in custody. His supervision lasts for five months (until the three-quarter point) and he remains at risk until his Sentence Expiry Date.

Paddy Naughtie goes to a PRES hostel

Paddy Naughtie has almost completed a mandatory life sentence for the murder of a night watchman during the course of committing an armed robbery. He has made satisfactory progress, been transferred to open conditions and been given a provisional release date. Paddy is being moved to a PRES hostel for his final six months, which is the last hurdle before release on life licence. Before moving to the hostel Paddy joins a job club to help him conduct a job search and learn how to prepare a CV. During his time in the PRES hostel his release plan is devised in consultation with the Probation Service responsible for his life licence supervision. The period in the PRES hostel goes according to plan and Paddy works full-time during the day as a market gardener until his release. He then goes to live with his girlfriend's family, where he stayed on resettlement leave, and starts seeking work.

Nicola Harrington prepares for release

Nicola Harrington was 21 and pregnant when she was sentenced to 18 months imprisonment. When the baby was due she was transferred to a mother-and-baby unit. Eventually the baby was placed with foster parents as she has no family to care for the child and no home to return to on release. Nicola recognises she will need considerable help and support after release and views positively the 4½-month period of statutory supervision by the Probation Service. Her probation officer obtains accommodation for her on release with the help of a Housing Association and she is discharged with a homeless rate discharge grant. The Benefits Agency are approached for help and she also makes an application for Housing Benefit to the local Council. Nicola consults the Benefits Agency booklet *Prisoners and their Families – a Guide to Benefits* and discovers that she is eligible for a range of benefits including a Community Care Grant.

CHECKLIST

- What is the National Throughcare Framework?
- When should an application be made for a discharge grant?
- How can offending behaviour be addressed?
- What are the aims of Inmate Development and Pre-Release courses?
- How can helplines assist prisoners?

- Who is eligible for repatriation to their own country?
- What is cognitive skills training?
- Identify the five stages in the Sex Offender Treatment Programme.
- What modules are included in Inmate Development and Pre-Release courses?
- Describe the role of a job club.
- Who receives a standard discharge grant?

- How can a Pre-Release Employment Scheme hostel help a long-term prisoner?
- What are Training and Enterprise Councils?
- How long does supervision after discharge last?
- What is a spent conviction?
- What does 'at risk' in the community mean?
- What is the rehabilitation period for a young offender serving six months in custody?
- How long is the 'registration period' for an adult convicted of a sexual offence?

DISCUSSION POINTS

1. Consider whether offending behaviour treatment programmes can counter the effects of eroding conditions.

2. 'The Relapse Prevention Programme recognises that Sex Offender Treatment Programmes cannot completely cure offenders.' Discuss.

3. Examine ways in which supervision in the community by the Probation Service can be improved.

4. After release, ex-offenders face enormous problems finding work. Examine how the Rehabilitation of Offenders Act can help to counter prejudice.

5. Consider the arguments for and against repatriating prisoners to their own country.

6. 'The complexities of the benefit system make it very difficult for ex-offenders to claim their entitlements on release.' Discuss.

CHAPTER 10

Serving a Life Sentence

TYPES OF LIFE SENTENCE

Anyone found guilty of murder automatically receives a life sentence, known as a *mandatory life sentence*. A life sentence is an indeterminate sentence: there is no guarantee of release, but if it is eventually approved the offender remains on life licence for the rest of their life.

The courts can sentence an offender to a *discretionary life sentence* for certain other offences. These include armed robbery, arson, manslaughter, attempted murder, rape, wounding with intent and causing an explosion. Such a sentence is imposed to reflect the seriousness of the offence or because the offender poses a serious risk to the public and it is doubtful whether they could safely be released at the end of a determinate sentence.

Anyone under the age of 18 convicted of murder is detained during Her Majesty's Pleasure (HMP). The original thinking behind HMP was to avoid the possibility of children facing the death penalty for murder. In practice young persons convicted of murder are treated as if they had received a mandatory life sentence.

The equivalent of a discretionary life sentence for a youngster under the age of 18 is called *detention for life*.

Custody for life is the equivalent of a mandatory life sentence for someone convicted of murder who is 18 or over, but under 21 when the offence was committed. A custody-for-life sentence can be passed on a young person for any other offence, where the court considers had they been dealing with an adult they would have received a life sentence.

A offender who is suffering from a mental disorder, as defined in Section 1 of the Mental Health Act 1983, can be detained as an alternative to prison in a Special Hospital or a secure psychiatric facility.

SECTION 2 DISCRETIONARIES

The Crime (Sentences) Act 1997 introduced an additional category of mandatory life sentence prisoner. Under Section 2 of the Act, anyone over the age of 18 who is convicted of a second serious violent or sexual offence after October 1997, the date the legislation came into force, can expect to receive a mandatory life sentence. Those sentenced under Section 2 of the Act are treated as a discretionary lifer and known as *Section 2 discretionaries*.

The tariff or minimum sentence to be served is decided by the court after it has considered the requirements of retribution and deterrence. All decisions about release on life licence are taken by the Parole Board at oral hearings and not by the Home Secretary.

There may be considerable variations in the length of tariffs that apply to Section 2 discretionaries. This could result in those held on remand for lengthy periods being entitled to an oral Parole Board review shortly after sentence. For these reasons all sentenced Section 2 discretionaries are being sent to one of the five main lifer centres:

- Wakefield.
- Wormword Scrubs.
- Gartree.
- Long Lartin.
- Brixton, which is concentrating on those with a short tariff.

THE TARIFF SYSTEM

A mandatory lifer is a person who is sentenced to life imprisonment custody for life, or detention at Her Majesty's Pleasure. The Secretary of State decides on the *tariff* for mandatory lifers. The tariff is that portion of the sentence which must be served to meet the public requirement for:

- retribution
- deterrence.

The tariff does not take into account issues like the 'risk of re-offending' as this is considered by the Parole Board. The question of 'public acceptability' falls within the responsibility of the Home Secretary after the Parole Board decide to recommend the release of a mandatory life sentence prisoner.

In the case of a discretionary lifer the *relevant part* of the sentence, also known as the tariff, is set by the trial judge in open court at the time of sentencing. This is the time that must be served in custody to meet the requirements of retribution and deterrence. In exceptional circumstances the judge may decline in open court to set a 'relevant part' of the sentence under Section 34 of the Criminal Justice Act 1991. This means the case is treated as if it were a mandatory life sentence.

The tariff for mandatory lifers is set by the Secretary of State after consulting the trial judge and the Lord Chief Justice. Although the views of the judiciary are considered to be very important, the final decision about the length of tariff rests with the Minister.

Ministers have made it clear that certain categories of murder will result in a minimum term of 20 years imprisonment. These include the murder of the following:

- police;
- prison officers;
- terrorist murder;
- murder in the course of an armed robbery;
- the sexual and sadistic murder of a child.

The process of setting the tariff involves the following:

- *The trial judge* gives an initial opinion.
- *The Lord Chief Justice* offers his advice to the Home Secretary.
- *The prisoner* is advised of the tariff together with the views of the trial judge and the Lord Chief Justice by the Tariff Unit of the Parole and Lifer Review Group.
- *The prisoner can make representations* to the Secretary of State within two months of being formally notified.
- *The Home Secretary* decides on the tariff and advises the prisoner of his decision together with the reasons.

Lifers with a *whole life* tariff are reviewed by Ministers after 25 years have elapsed and subsequently every five years, in order to assess the risk to the public. The purpose of the review is to consider the appropriateness of amending the whole life tariff to a fixed term.

An important judgment affecting tariff setting for young persons sentenced to be detained during Her Majesty's Pleasure (HMP) under Section 53(1) of the Children and Young Person's Act 1933 was the House of Lords ruling on 12 June 1997 (ex parte T & V). The judgment established the principle that the initial view of what is necessary by way of retribution and deterrence should be capable of reduction in the light of the offender's personal development while in custody, and that the offender's personal development should be considered alongside the public interest in retribution and deterrence in keeping the tariff period under review.

Since this ruling the Home Secretary has introduced the following changes:

- all HMPs whose original tariff has not expired are reviewed annually;
- Ministers comprehensively review all cases halfway through the original tariff period and consider representations from the young person;
- all those serving HMP are advised of the Minister's Statement dated 10 November 1997, including their right to request a review at any time.

MANAGING LIFERS

The career of an adult male life sentence prisoner generally progresses through a number of stages:

Local prison
- All newly sentenced lifers are security categorised.
- The initial life sentence report is prepared.
- The tariff-setting process commences for mandatory lifers.
- All lifers convicted of a sex-related offence or with a history of sexual offending are identified for transfer to HMP Wakefield to be assessed for the sex offender treatment programme (SOTP).
- Lifers are allocated to a Main Centre by the *Lifer Management Unit* (LMU).

Main Centre

- Lifers normally spend about three years in a Main Centre.
- The initial assessment is completed and the *Life Sentence Plan* is completed with any special needs highlighted.
- The first *F75 reports* are requested by the Lifer Management Unit after the lifer has spent about 2½ years in prison.
- Lifers who are disruptive and present control or disciplinary problems can be transferred to different establishments other than those envisaged in the Life Sentence Plan.

Category B training or dispersal establishment

- The main part of the sentence is served in at least one Category B establishment.
- The life sentence plan is embarked on including addressing identified offending behaviour.
- Once there is evidence of significant progress, the Lifer Allocations Unit can consider a move to Category C conditions.

Category C establishments

- A move to Category C conditions does not normally take place until the date of the first Parole Board Review is less than three years away.
- The focus on addressing offending behaviour moves towards preparation for release on life licence.
- Eligible inmates are considered for local town visits.

Category D Open Conditions

- Subject to the approval of the Minister, most lifers progress to open conditions where the potential risk to the public can be carefully assessed and tested out, before release on licence is considered.
- This may involve a period at a resettlement prison such as Latchmere House or Kirklevington Grange.
- Category D conditions provide opportunities for supervised outside activities.

Pre-release Employment Scheme (PRES)

- Normally a lifer spends 6–9 months at a PRES hostel or a Resettlement Prison.
- PRES provides an opportunity to gain work experience under realistic conditions resembling what the lifer will experience on release.
- Regular progress reports are prepared by the Hostel Warden for the Parole and Lifer Review Group (PLRG).
- The outside supervising probation officer also prepares reports for PLRG.

WOMEN AND FEMALE YOUNG OFFENDERS

The career of a female lifer is similar in principle to that of a sentenced male, although the range of options is more limited due to the size of the estate. There are only 14 female establishments, five of which are units located within male establishments.

Apart from the high-risk women who are categorised A, women are either categorised as suitable for open conditions or closed conditions. Female young offenders and women are kept in the same establishments. Some young offenders commence their sentence in a Secure Unit run by the Social Services Department before being transferred to the penal system when they are 18 years old.

The two main centres for women are at Durham and Bullwood Hall, where inmates normally remain to be assessed until the first F75 reports have been completed. In common with male offenders they spend up to three years at a Main Centre. Women who require full-time medical care can remain at Holloway, or be transferred there at any stage in their sentence.

The second stage of a woman's sentence is spent at another closed establishment where work continues to address offending behaviour and other identified needs.

The third and final stage of the sentence is served in open conditions where inmates can be tested and can take part in supervised outside activities.

MALE YOUNG OFFENDERS

Young male offenders are not categorised in the same way as adults until they move into the adult system at around 18 years of age. The four main centres for young persons are at Aylesbury, Castington, Moorland and Swinfen Hall.

Section 53 of the Children and Young Persons Act 1933 gives the Secretary of State discretion to decide where to detain a young person as follows:

- a children's home run by the Social Services Department;
- Glenthorne Youth Treatment Centre run by the Department of Health's Youth Treatment Service;
- a Young Offender Institution.

A juvenile sentenced to detention during Her Majesty's Pleasure under Section 53(1) may begin his sentence in a Secure Unit run by the Social Services Department if he is not placed in a YOI.

Normally by the time they are 18 years old juveniles are transferred to a Young Offender Institution. If not, they must be transferred to an adult establishment before they are 22 years old.

The first review occurs shortly after the young offender lifer is received into custody. The aim is to identify any immediate needs, allocate the young person to an appropriate wing or unit, and then decide on a suitable work or educational programme.

The first formal internal review takes place six months after reception into a YOI, by which time the inmate should have settled into the regime. The purpose of the review is to devise a training plan following a full assessment of personal and training needs, which includes a programme that addresses offending behaviour.

The second internal review, following six months later, aims to reassess the training plan, review progress achieved towards the agreed targets, and consider when the young person should be transferred to an adult system. The progression to the adult system normally takes place when the inmate is between 21 and 22 years old. Those who have spent three years in a main long-term YOI are normally transferred to a

Category B or Category C prison, depending on when the first review is due. Some youngsters may spend a short period in a Main Centre before their transfer to a Category B or Category C prison takes place. It all depends on achieving satisfactory reports and the date of the first Parole Board review.

A young person who makes good progress through the system can take part in a range of supervised outside activities. Once they have been given a provisional release date they are eligible to be considered for all forms of release on temporary licence, and this can be as early as four months after transfer to open conditions.

Anyone who has not received a provisional release date but has been in open conditions for six months can be considered for release under a compassionate licence should the need arise. After nine months in open conditions a young person is eligible to be considered for a resettlement licence.

There are three types of temporary licence:

- Compassionate Licence.
- Facility Licence.
- Resettlement Licence.

The principles governing release on licences and the criteria that apply are covered in the section 'Release on temporary licence' (see page 51).

THE LIFE SENTENCE PLAN

The *Life Sentence Plan* is an ongoing record of the progress of a lifer in custody. It is an important document which is used to manage the life sentence, and enables a consistent approach to be taken throughout the lifer's time in custody.

A Life Sentence Plan is prepared for every lifer irrespective of their age and gender. It applies to discretionary, mandatory and Category A lifers. A detailed risk assessment is prepared, then offending behaviour needs to be identified and addressed and strategies devised to tackle the problems.

The Life Sentence Plan includes all the annual review board progress reports and the annual sentence plan summary for the next twelve months. In line with the policy of open reporting, these are shared with the lifer.

The following professional staff contribute to the process:

- Seconded probation officer.
- Education Co-ordinator.
- Psychiatrist.
- Psychologist.
- Medical Officer.
- Chaplain.

These reports are in addition to prison reports prepared by:

- Personal prison officer.
- Wing manager.
- Governor with responsibility for life sentence prisoners.

Other staff with knowledge about the individual may also contribute:

- Physical education officer.
- Workshop instructor.
- Catering officer.

At the end of the initial 12-month period the Lifer Review Board complete a Sentence Plan Summary which identifies:

- agreed targets to address offending behaviour;
- specialist groups or programmes that will help achieve this objective;
- the frequency that information about the risk assessment will be collated and reviewed. This is usually at three-monthly intervals;
- how identified needs can be met through attending work, education and recreational activities;
- agreed long-term targets for later in the sentence, which are dependent on satisfactory progress being maintained;
- any other recommendations or comments from the Lifer Review Board.

It is important to involve each lifer fully in the process which includes devising and setting targets. They should be given the opportunity to contribute and comment on progress they have achieved, and be invited to attend at least part of the Lifer Review Board.

THE LIFE SENTENCE REVIEW

Comprehensive reports are compiled on lifers throughout their sentence. The main types of reviews are as follows.

Internal reviews

Each prison holding lifers must have a *Lifer Review Board* to thoroughly review all life sentence cases every twelve months. Representatives from all relevant departments in the establishment attend the review and contribute reports. The Lifer Review Board prepare the Life Sentence Plan soon after the lifer arrives at the Main Centre, and update it each year.

Reviewing Category A lifers

Each year the security classification of Category A prisoners is reviewed. In the case of a Category A lifer the annual review and any F75 reports due for completion are prepared at the same time.

Interim F75 reviews

A comprehensive set of reports, known as F75 reports, are produced every three years up until the date of the first Parole Board Review. Thereafter, F75 reports may be required where the interval between Parole Board Reviews exceeds three years. The purpose of interim reports is to monitor progress, and review the security category and need for a transfer to another establishment. The outcome of an interim review is disclosed to the lifer, who has the right to see the contents of their Parole Board dossiers including the F75 reports. The initial F75 report is compiled towards the end of their time at the main lifer centre. These reports determine where the next stage of their sentence will be served, as decisions reached by the Lifer Management Unit are based on these reports. Some lifers may move on to Category C conditions, while others are transferred to a Category B training prison. The decisions of the Parole Board are influenced by the following:

(a) custodial behaviour;
(b) the degree of risk they pose to the public;
(c) to what extent they have come to terms with their offence and offending behaviour;
(d) whether any remorse is evident;
(e) how much of the tariff they have left to serve.

The Ministerial Review at ten years

Since 1994 the Home Secretary has conducted a review of each mandatory life sentence prisoner after ten years in custody. The purpose of the ten-year Ministerial review is to consider whether there any grounds for bringing forward the date of the first review by the Parole Board.

The Parole Board Review

A Parole Board Review takes place three years before the expiry of the tariff or 'relevant part' of the sentence and applies to mandatory and discretionary life sentence prisoners. The review date can be deferred if an escape or abscond occurs, or if a further custodial sentence were to be received. A discretionary lifer who has reached his tariff date would be unaffected by a further sentence as he is entitled to a Discretionary Lifer Panel review every two years.

The parole dossier compiled for the Parole Board contains the following:

* reports from every establishment that has held the lifer;
* Home Office Summary about the circumstances of the offence and psychiatric reports produced at the time of the trial.

The lifer can make representations to the Parole Board, or use his solicitor under the Green Form Scheme to make them on his behalf. After the Parole Board have considered all the establishment reports, as well as relevant external reports (for example, if offences against children have been committed, a report from the Social Services Department will be included), they will weigh up the risk of further offences being committed after release, and the likelihood of the inmate abiding by conditions of life licence and co-operating with the supervising probation officer. The Parole Board's recommendations are advisory so have to be approved by the Home Secretary.

The Parole Board can recommend any of the following:

(a) *No further progress*
(b) *A move to open conditions*
   Any recommendation has to receive Ministerial approval.
(c) *The release of a mandatory life sentence prisoner*
   The Home Secretary must personally approve the recommendation of the Parole
   Board and set the provisional release date. The Parole Board provide reasons for any
   decision, which are disclosed to the lifer. They recommend the date for the next
   review, which is normally a minimum of two years, and highlight any areas of concern that need to be addressed in the meantime.

The Ministerial Review at 25 years

Lifers who are to remain in prison for the rest of their natural life do not receive a Parole
Board Review. Since 1994 the Minister has held an additional review after imprisonment for 25 years, and every five years thereafter, to consider if the need for retribution
and deterrence has been met, and whether there are any valid reasons for converting
the whole life tariff to one of a determinate period.

DISCRETIONARY LIFER PANELS

The Parole Board Rules 1997 set out how *Discretionary Lifer Panel* hearings are to be conducted. The main effect of these changes is to introduce arrangements for all
discretionary lifers to have an oral hearing, including the new category of *Section 2 discretionaries* and anyone detained during Her Majesty's Pleasure.

Each discretionary lifer case is reviewed six months before the tariff date by the
Parole Board. The Chairman of the Parole Board appoints three members of the Board
to form a Discretionary Lifer Panel which comprises:

* a circuit judge or recorder who acts as Chairman;
* a psychiatrist;
* a probation officer or an independent panel member.

A High Court judge chairs the Discretionary Lifer Panel when the most serious
cases are being considered, as in the case of offences of:

* terrorism;
* serial rape;
* attempted murder;
* the sexual assault and murder of a child;
* offences involving more than one life sentence.

The Discretionary Lifer Panel lists each case and notifies the prisoner 23 weeks
prior to the hearing of the procedure and the right to be represented. A prisoner cannot be represented by a serving prisoner, anyone who is on licence, or someone who
is liable to be detained under the Mental Health Act 1983, or anyone with an unspent
conviction for an imprisonable offence.

The procedures and timetable for the proceedings are set out in The Parole Board Rules 1997 and are as follows:

- *Five weeks' notice* has to be given by the lifer if he wishes to be represented, and he should provide details of his representative.
- *Twelve weeks' notice* has to be given to call witnesses and the prisoner must include the substance of the evidence he proposes to rely on.
- *Fifteen weeks* in advance of the hearing any representations the lifer wishes to have considered must be received by the Board. Any other supporting documentation has to be provided within 14 days of the date of the hearing.

Apart from any *withheld* evidence all the documents that comprise the parole dossier can be disclosed to the prisoner eight weeks before the hearing. The parole dossier includes the following documents:

- personal information about the prisoner;
- papers relating to the offence;
- the Life Sentence Plan;
- summaries of previously submitted reports from earlier reviews;
- comprehensive and up-to-date prison reports which include:
  (a) a report from the establishment's Lifer Liaison Officer, who is the Governor with responsibility for lifers;
  (b) Wing Manager;
  (c) Personal Officer;
  (d) Education Co-ordinator (if applicable);
  (e) Chaplain (if applicable);
  (f) Medical Officer, (and if appropriate a psychiatric report);
  (g) Psychologist's report (where possible);
  (h) home Probation Officer who can report on the home circumstances, employ- ment prospects, the views of the victim, and any public concerns affecting release on licence;
  (i) the prisoner's written representations.

Unless the panel chairman decides to hold a preliminary hearing, everyone is given 21 days notice of the date of the hearing. The hearing normally takes place in the establishment where the lifer is being held and is conducted in private, in an informal manner, and the evidence is treated as confidential.

The panel chairman explains the procedures to be followed in the hearing, hears the evidence of witnesses, allows an opportunity for questions to be put, and gives the prisoner and his representative the opportunity to address the panel.

The chairman considers any 'withheld' evidence – documentation withheld from the prisoner on the grounds that their disclosure would, in the opinion of the Secretary of State, adversely affect the health and welfare of the prisoner or another person. If the lifer has chosen a representative who is a barrister, a registered medical practitioner or a suitably qualified person, they can see the evidence provided it is treated in the strictest of confidence and not disclosed to the prisoner without the permission of the chairman of the panel.

Provided the majority of the panel members are in agreement, that majority decision is acted upon. Any recommendations concerning a move to open conditions are subject to Ministerial approval.

All decisions are formally recorded and are communicated to all concerned, together with the reasons, within seven days of the hearing.

ESCORTED ABSENCES

Once a lifer has progressed satisfactorily and is suitable for Category C conditions the emphasis of offence-related work shifts towards resettlement.

Approval for an escorted absence can only be given for a lifer whose behaviour in the establishment gives no cause for concern, and who is making good progress in tackling his offending behaviour. To qualify he must be a Category C prisoner who has been risk assessed and able to co-operate with a prison officer without resorting to the use of handcuffs.

An escorted absence acts as a powerful incentive and is allowed in recognition that good progress has been achieved. Escorted absences allow a lifer to visit places of interest, use public transport, get used to the traffic, adjust to the pressures of life outside, make purchases in shops and obtain refreshments including a snack meal.

It provides an opportunity for staff to assess whether the lifer can take responsibility for his own behaviour, to gauge his reaction to women and children and test out his ability to resist the pressure from others including the temptation to smuggle unauthorised items into the prison.

An escorted absence can only take place with the approval of the *Lifer Management Unit* in Prison Service Headquarters. It must meet the following criteria laid down for escorted absences which excludes attending a sporting or charitable event, or a social occasion:

- staff are confident the lifer will not escape;
- they are well behaved;
- the individual has made good progress in addressing his offending behaviour;
- he does not pose a danger to the public;
- he is not subject to a Deportation Order;
- a parole review is due within 12 months and he is less than four years from the tariff date;
- the victim has been consulted under the terms of the Victim's Charter 1996;
- in the case of Schedule 1 offenders the Social Services Department have raised no concerns;
- the Police, the Probation Service and the establishment all support the application.

Escorted absences are subject to the following conditions:

(a) they are limited to six hours;
(b) a maximum of three absences can be approved in a year;

(c) they must be taken within two months of approval;
(d) visits to relatives and home visits are not permitted.

Once the visit has taken place a report is compiled detailing the lifer's response to the privilege, and this forms part of their dossier.

THE MENTALLY DISORDERED LIFER

A mentally disordered offender serving a life sentence can be transferred to hospital under the Mental Health Act 1983. The life sentence continues to be served but the inmate cannot be considered for release until the tariff or 'relevant' part of the sentence has been served.

The Mental Health Unit in the Home Office manages all lifers committed to hospital and their cases are reviewed by a *Mental Health Review Tribunal*.

The Home Secretary can authorise the transfer of a lifer to hospital for treatment under Section 47 of the Mental Health Act 1983. This warrant, known as a *transfer direction*, can be exercised if two doctors, one of whom is an approved doctor under Section 12 of the Act, diagnose that the lifer is suffering from any of the following conditions and needs to be treated in hospital:

• mental illness;
• a psychopathic disorder;
• severe mental impairment or mental impairment.

A *restriction direction* enables a lifer to be returned to prison if his condition improves before the date of release calculated while he was in prison. The aim is to make sure prisoners are not released earlier than if they had remained in prison.

Once the date of release arrives these restrictions do not apply, although if the prisoner still needs treatment he can be detained on a hospital order under Section 37 of the Mental Health Act 1983.

The Mental Health Review Tribunal

Anyone transferred from prison to hospital can apply to have their case reviewed within six months of the 'transfer direction' and each year following that review. If they do not request a review while in hospital, their case is automatically referred to the tribunal by the Home Office after three years have elapsed.

The Tribunal cannot authorise the release of a prisoner detained in hospital but can advise the Home Secretary about the need for further detention in hospital.

Once the Tribunal concludes a patient no longer requires treatment in hospital or his condition cannot be satisfactorily treated, it is normal practice to return him to prison to complete their sentence. The time spent in hospital under these circumstances counts towards his sentence.

In 1994 the Court of Appeal decided that discretionary and mandatory life sentence prisoners admitted to hospital under the Mental Health Act 1983 remain prisoners, and do not have the right to have their cases reviewed by the Parole Board.

Irrespective of whether they remain in hospital or return to prison, until the Secretary of State is satisfied they no longer need medical treatment or cannot be treated effectively, their cases cannot be referred to the Parole Board.

Once a lifer returns to prison the Parole Board review process can commence.

The first review is normally held three years before the tariff date. This takes place in the normal way if the lifer returns to prison and there is sufficient time to assess progress since he was treated in hospital. Otherwise the review may be deferred for up to a year following his return to prison in order to allow time to assess progress, prepare comprehensive reports, and complete a risk assessment.

A discretionary life sentence prisoner who has completed the tariff or relevant part of the sentence by the time he returns to prison can have his case referred to the Parole Board who will set a date for the Discretionary Lifer Panel Hearing.

LIFER THROUGHCARE

An inmate serving a life sentence will be in contact with the Probation Service for the rest of his life. Supervision commences when they are on remand and continues until after they are eventually released back into the community on life licence supervision.

The *home probation officer* is involved in the preparation of court reports and continues contact as the primary worker until sentence is pronounced.

The *seconded probation officer* is the primary worker while the lifer is in custody and contributes progress reports on a regular basis including the Lifer Sentence Planning Process. They are closely involved in identifying and addressing offending behaviour and play an active role in preparations for release.

After release the primary worker becomes the *supervising probation officer* with responsibility for supervising the life licence, monitoring the lifer's behaviour, safeguarding the risk to the public, and acting accordingly if there are grounds for revocation of the licence and recall to prison.

Initially the role of the probation officer is to provide advice to the court, the lifer, his family, the victim and their family. The probation officer prepares a *pre-sentence report* in the case of each discretionary lifer, which is sent to the Prison Governor, the Lifer Management Unit and the seconded probation officer.

Once a sentence of life imprisonment has been passed, the home probation officer prepares a *post-sentence report* which is used in the preparation of the Life Sentence Plan. This report is prepared within three months of sentence and forms part of the dossier compiled for formal reviews.

The post sentence report is wide-ranging and covers in depth the following aspects:

- the circumstances of the offence;
- advice on the risk assessment and the level of danger the individual poses to the public;
- any history of a pattern of offending behaviour, including any alcohol or drug abuse;
- any significant medical history and relationship difficulties within the family;
- his attitude to the offence;
- how family members feel and have reacted to his offending;
- any adverse local feeling or hostility including that of the victim's relatives.

During the custodial part of the sentence the seconded probation officer contributes actively to the Life Sentence Plan, reviews by the Parole Board, and in detailed preparations made for their release.

Once a provisional release date has been notified, a supervising probation officer is nominated in the area that the lifer intends to live on release. Most lifers spend between six and nine months on a Pre-Release Employment Scheme (PRES) and some attend a PRES hostel. The supervising probation officer takes an increasingly prominent and significant role in the resettlement arrangements as the provisional date of release approaches.

Close liaison between the establishment and the supervising probation officer ensures that any developments likely to affect the release plans are shared. If behaviour becomes a source of concern, or disciplinary action becomes necessary, this can result in the provisional release date being deferred or withdrawn altogether.

On release a lifer remains subject to the terms and conditions of life licence and can be recalled for the remainder of his natural life, in the case of a mandatory life sentenced prisoner.

THE VICTIM'S CHARTER

The Victim's Charter 1996 places a duty on the Probation Service to provide information and advice to victims and take into account their concerns when making plans to resettle a life sentence prisoner.

These requirements have been incorporated into the National Standards of the Probation Service and involve making contact with the victim and their family within two months of the date of sentence and providing information about the following:

- the life sentence custodial process;
- the time-scale affecting likely consideration for temporary release and discharge from prison;
- the arrangements for life licence supervision;
- the sentence management process;
- the key stages in the sentence when the views and concerns of the victim and their family are actively considered, particularly as decisions could impact on them.

The key stages in the sentence when contact with all victims is made are as follows:

- at the interim F75 stage;
- when the Parole Board review stage is reached;
- when escorted absences and temporary release are being considered;
- at the point where a move to open conditions or a PRES hostel is being contemplated.

The Victim's Charter places a duty on the Probation Service to take the victim's concerns fully into consideration when making plans. This does not mean a victim has the power of veto regarding the release of a lifer on life licence.

However, the victim's concerns can lead to conditions being imposed which allay their anxieties and safeguard their interests. Victims are not allowed to be told personal information about the lifer such as their date of release, their discharge address, or even the area they are planning to settle in. This guards against any possibility of the victim and their family being tempted to take the law into their own hands and seek retribution.

Victim support groups play an important role in providing mutual support for victims of serious crime. Probation officers are in contact with local victim support schemes and can make the necessary introductions.

LIFE LICENCE AND RECALL

A mandatory life sentence prisoner can be released by the Home Secretary on the recommendation of the Parole Board, after he has consulted the Lord Chief Justice and the original trial judge, if available. The Home Secretary has to be satisfied that the following criteria have been fully met:

* the period served by the lifer is adequate to meet the requirements of retribution and deterrence;
* the individual is safe for release;
* early release on licence is acceptable to public opinion.

Before releasing a discretionary life sentence prisoner the Secretary of State has to be satisfied the following conditions have been met:

* the 'relevant part' of the sentence has been served;
* the Parole Board have authorised release;
* the Parole Board are satisfied there is no further value in keeping an individual in custody in order to protect the public.

The Secretary of State can release a lifer on compassionate grounds in exceptional circumstances, under Section 36 of the Criminal Justice Act 1991. He can only exercise this discretion, after consulting the Parole Board, where there is medical evidence confirming the individual is suffering from a terminal illness, and their life expectancy is limited.

Once it has been decided to release a lifer, the Chief Probation Officer of the area to which the lifer is being released will be informed. He will be sent the following documents:

* a copy of the life licence (see p. 177 for specimen copy of male life licence);
* the final risk assessment;
* the most recent Parole Board dossier;
* details of work undertaken to address their offending behaviour, which was included in the Life Sentence plan;
* any remaining areas of concern.

The National Identification Bureau at New Scotland Yard is kept updated on all lifer movements. It is advised of the release date and discharge address of all those released on life licence.

The Probation Service is responsible for supervising the lifer on life licence. This supervision is at a level consistent with the 'National Standards for Supervision Before and After Release from Custody' and involves keeping in contact through regular office interviews, home visits and telephone contact.

Immediately following release this contact takes place weekly for the first month and includes paying a home visit. This level of contact gradually reduces to fortnightly visits until three months after release when monthly contact becomes the norm, provided no concerns have been identified and there is a positive response to contact.

Any change of address has to be agreed with, and notified to, the supervising probation officer who advises both the police and the Parole & Lifer Review Group (PLRG) in Prison Service Headquarters.

RECALL

A mandatory life sentence prisoner once released has to comply with the terms and conditions of his life licence, otherwise he is liable to recall. Any life licence can be revoked by the Home Secretary on the recommendation of the Parole Board.

Under Section 39(2) of the Criminal Justice Act 1991, the Secretary of State has the power to immediately recall a licensee without consulting the Parole Board where it is clearly in the public interest to act promptly. In the event of recall the case must be referred to the Parole Board for confirmation of the decision.

There does not have to be a prosecution and conviction for a further offence before recalling a licensee. Concern about drug-taking, alcohol abuse or anti-social behaviour may be sufficient to justify action on the grounds that there is a risk to the public of the licensee committing further serious offences.

The following are all grounds for the recall of a lifer:

- any significant changes in domestic arrangements;
- a deterioration in mental health;
- a failure to maintain contact with the supervising probation officer;
- any breaches of the conditions of licence.

The overriding priority is to ensure the safety of the public and that no person is put in jeopardy in any way.

Maintaining the correct balance between the interests of the individual lifer and the risk to the community, the courts have ruled, is the responsibility of the Secretary of State and the Parole Board.

The Parole Board considers all recommendations to recall a licensee. Before recalling a mandatory life sentence prisoner the Parole Board takes into account the views of the supervising probation officer, the recommendations of the Chief Probation Officer, and weighs up the following factors:

- the risk to the safety of other people;
- the likelihood of further imprisonable offences being committed;

- any failure to comply with the conditions of licence;
- any unwillingness to co-operate with the supervising probation officer.

The most frequent reasons for recalling a licensee are when criminal charges are brought, or when the supervising probation officer reports a failure to keep to the conditions of the life licence.

If the life licence is revoked, the licensee has to return to prison to continue serving the sentence. They are entitled to a detailed explanation of the reasons for the revocation of the life licence, and are given the opportunity to seek legal advice and make representations to the Parole Board.

After considering their representations the Parole Board can direct that a discretionary lifer should be immediately released.

In the case of a mandatory lifer the Parole Board can only recommend their release. In practice any recommendation or direction by the Parole Board under these circumstances is binding on the Secretary of State under section 39(5) of the Criminal Justice Act 1991.

In the event that the recall and subsequent review by the Parole Board does not result in immediate release, the Secretary of State has to decide on the timing of the next review.

The subsequent review of a discretionary lifer is handled by a Discretionary Lifer Panel, whereas the review of a mandatory lifer is considered by the Parole Board.

CASE STUDY

Paddy Naughtie is released on life licence

Paddy Naughtie received a mandatory life sentence for the murder of a night watchman during the course of an armed robbery 8 years ago. Prior to release on life licence he spent six months in a PRES hostel which he completed without incident. On release the conditions of life licence were explained to him and he set up home with his girlfriend in her council flat. He managed to obtain work in a local garden centre and for the first twelve months Paddy appeared to be settling back into the community satisfactorily. The relationship began to run into difficulties and eventually broke down, so Paddy moved out into lodgings, with the agreement of his supervising probation officer. With both parents dead, no family ties remaining, and few friends, Paddy began mixing with the criminal fraternity. He soon became involved in the local drug scene and evidence that Paddy was taking and supplying drugs came to light. A drug raid uncovered a quantity of class A drugs amongst his possessions and he was charged with possession. This information was brought to the attention of the Home Secretary who decided to recall Paddy immediately under section 39(2) of the Criminal Justice Act 1991 and he was returned to prison. Paddy lodged an appeal to the Parole Board, but this was rejected after he was convicted and sentenced to five years imprisonment. The Parole Board notified Paddy that his case would not be reviewed for three years.

CHECKLIST

- What is a mandatory life sentence?
- When does the Court impose a discretionary life sentence?
- Which prisoners are known as 'Section 2 discretionaries?'
- Who can be sentenced to 'detention for life?'
- What is the distinction between 'detention for life' and 'custody for life?'
- Who can be detained during Her Majesty's Pleasure?
- Where can a mentally disordered offender be held as an alternative to prison?

- How is the tariff set for a mandatory life sentence?
- What is the 'relevant part' of the sentence?
- When does the Minister review the case of a prisoner with a 'whole life' tariff?
- Who is responsible for managing life sentence prisoners?
- How is the Life Sentence Plan compiled?
- What is a F75 report?

- What is the membership of a Discretionary Lifer Panel?
- Who is entitled to an oral hearing?
- Why is certain evidence withheld from the parole dossier?
- When does a Mental Health Tribunal meet to review the case of a prisoner detained in hospital under the Mental Health Act 1983?
- Why would a 'transfer direction' warrant be obtained?'
- What is a 'restriction direction?'
- How is the supervising probation officer involved in the recall of a prisoner on life licence?

DISCUSSION POINTS

1. Serious offenders sentenced before the Criminal Justice Act 1991 was introduced are not released under compulsory supervision. How can public anxieties be allayed when convicted paedophiles are released into the community?

2. What steps should be taken to prevent a life sentence prisoner exploiting the notoriety of his case?

3. The public interest can best be served by sentencing convicted sex offenders to a discretionary life sentence. Discuss.

4. How can the needs of victims of crime be met more effectively?

5. 'Judges should have the right to set a lesser term than a mandatory life sentence for a murderer who they believe deserves more lenient treatment.' Discuss.

6. How can the process of deciding the relevant part of the sentence for a discretionary life sentence prisoner be improved?

APPENDIX I

Documents

MANDATORY DRUG TEST AUTHORISATION FORM

Prisoner Name: ....   **Number:** ....

> Test Reference Number:
>
>
>
>
>
> *For allocation when sample is collected*

1. The governor has authorised that in accordance with Section 16A of the Prison Act 1952 any prisoner may be required by a prison officer to provide a sample of urine for the purposes of testing for the presence of a controlled drug.

2. You are now required under the terms of Section 16A to provide a fresh and unadulterated sample of urine for testing for the presence of controlled drugs.

3. Authority for this requirement was given by: ....

4. Reason for requirement: (only one box to be ticked)

    [ ] **Random test:** You have been selected for this test on a strictly random basis.

    [ ] **Reasonable suspicion:** You have been selected for this test because staff have reason to believe that you have misused drugs. This test has been approved by a senior manager.

    [ ] **Risk assessment:** You have been selected for this test because you are being considered for a privilege, or a job, where a high degree of trust is to be given to you.

    [ ] **Frequent test programme:** You have been selected for more frequent testing because of your previous history of drug misuse.

    [ ] **On reception:** You have been selected for testing on reception on a random basis.

5. The procedures used during the collection and testing of the sample have been designed to protect you and to ensure that there are no mistakes in the handling of your sample. At the end of the collection procedure you will be asked to sign a statement confirming that the urine sealed in the sample bottles for testing is fresh and your own.

6. Your sample will be split at the point of collection into separate containers which will be sealed in your presence. In the event of you disputing any positive test result, one of these containers will be available, for a period of up to 12 months, for you to arrange, if you so wish, for an independent analysis to be undertaken at your own expense.

7. You will be liable to be placed on report if you:

    (a)   provide a positive sample;
    (b)   refuse to provide a sample; or,
    (c)   fail to provide a sample after 4 hours of the order to do so (or after 5 hours if the officer believes that you are experiencing real difficulty in providing a sample).

Consent to Medical disclosure

*   (i)   During the past 30 days I have not used any medication issued to me by Health Care.

*   (ii)   During the past 30 days I have used medication issued to me by Health Care. I understand that some medication issued by Health Care may affect the result of the test. I give my consent to the Medical Officer to provide details of this treatment to the prison authorities.

(*Delete as appropriate)

Signature of Prisoner : ....   **Date:** ....

MDTA/12/95

PRISON SERVICE CHAIN OF CUSTODY PROCEDURE

Prisoner Name: .... Number: ....

NON-RANDOM TESTING PROGRAMME (Tick box on tear-off section to indicate reason for test)

Checklist for sample collection - tick boxes as you proceed. Refer to guidance notes if in doubt.

1 [ ] Only **One** sample collection kit present.
2 [ ] Check identity of prisoner. Complete details above and in sample collection register.
3 [ ] Carry out search and handwashing procedures. (No soap).
4 [ ] Show the prisoner that the collection cup and bottles are empty.
5 [ ] Ask prisoner to provide enough urine to be split **equally** between the two sample bottles.
6 [ ] *When a temperature check is necessary, take temperature using a thermometer or temperature strip in accordance with the suppliers instructions. If temperature is out of range (32-38C) (90-100F), make note in comments section and refer to guidance notes.*
7 [ ] **Watched by prisoner,** transfer urine **equally** between the two bottles. **Press caps on securely.**
8 [ ] Ask prisoner to initial and date both bottle seals.
9 [ ] **Watched by prisoner,** place a seal over each bottle cap.
10 [ ] Dispose of any surplus urine and the cup.
11 [ ] Pack two bottles in mailing container and then in chain of custody bag - **Do not seal bag.**
12 [ ] **Watched by prisoner,** fix barcode labels and enter test reference number on all copies of this form.
13 [ ] Ask the prisoner to sign and date the Prisoner's Declaration below.
14 [ ] Complete Chain of Custody Report, tear off and place in chain of custody bag facing outwards.
15 [ ] Seal bag, ask prisoner to initial bag where indicated.
16 [ ] Place sealed bag in secure refrigerator until ready for despatch to laboratory.
17 [ ] Allow prisoner to leave.

Prisoner Declaration

I confirm that (i)   I understand why I was required to provide the sample and what may happen if I fail to comply with this requirement;
(ii) the urine sample I have given was my own and freshly provided;
(iii) the sample was divided into two bottles and sealed in my presence with seals initialled and dated by me;
(iv) the seals used on these bottles carry a barcode identical to the barcode attached to this form.

Signature of prisoner .... Date ....

(Tear off along perforation)

Comments

CHAIN OF CUSTODY REPORT

Reason for test *(tick 1 box)*: [ ] Suspicion: [ ] Frequent: [ ] Reception: [ ] Risk:

Collecting officer declaration

Name (Print) .... Prison ....
I confirm that the enclosed sample, bearing the Barcode identified below, was collected in accordance with the sample collection procedures agreed between the Prison Service and the laboratory.

Prisoners Sex *(tick 1 box)* [ ]M [ ] F   Prisoners Ethnic Code.................................. | Test Reference Number:

Sample collected on Date .... Time ....

Signature of Collecting officer .... | Barcode

For the information of the laboratory only | **NON RANDOM**

[ ]]

For laboratory use only

Name .... Signature .... Date .... Time ....

MDTLN/4/96

REQUEST/COMPLAINT FORM

THIS SECTION FOR OFFICIAL USE ONLY

ESTABLISHMENT HMP CAMPHILL			CATEGORY C	STATUS M	DATE ISSUED 16/10/98
NAME MILES			SERIAL No. 458/98		DATE RECEIVED 22/10/98
NUMBER XC4956	LOCATION B WING	DATE OF BIRTH 17-6-66	CROSS REF. —		DATE REPLIED 30/10/98

GUIDANCE NOTES:

(Further information is given in the booklet "How to make a request or complaint")

1. Please try to resolve your request/complaint informally if you can.

2. A written request/complaint should be made within 3 months of the relevant facts coming to your notice. A complaint about improper treatment should be made as soon as possible, giving full details. You should use this form within 3 months of the date issued.

3. Please limit your request/complaint to one subject. Ask for a separate form if there is something else you want to raise.

4. Please write clearly. Do not use abusive or insulting language.

5. Please write in ENGLISH if possible. (Welsh speaking inmates may write in Welsh). If you write in another language this could lead to delay.

HAVE YOU DISCUSSED YOUR REQUEST/COMPLAINT WITH ANYONE? IF SO. WHOM? Yes.

The Wing Governor who chaired the Restoration of Remission Board

REQUEST/COMPLAINT (give reasons where appropriate):

I wish to appeal against the Wing Governor's decision. His reasons for not giving me more time back are as follows:

"I have restored 28 days remission because you have kept clear of trouble for the past six months and this deserves to be recognised. I have taken into account your medical problems but feel that you must make a greater effort to find work".

(You may continue on the back if necessary)

WHAT ACTION WOULD YOU LIKE TAKEN?

I would like another 30 days back.

(Request/Complaint continued)

I do not agree with this and think it is unfair. I suffer with agoraphobia and this has made it difficult for me to find a suitable job. At my previous prison I worked as a wing cleaner and attended the gym every day. Since I've been at this prison I have gone to the gym every day and I help out on the wing from time to time and will continue to do so until a vacancy arises. I would like the other 30 days restored.

SIGNATURE: P. Miles   DATE: 20/10/98

REPLY:

I have reviewed your case and would remind you that restoring added days is not an entitlement but a privilege that has to be earned. The decision about how many to restore takes into account the nature of the disciplinary offences you committed, your overall performance based on the written reports compiled by staff together with your written application. You have had 116 days added to your sentence and are eligible to apply for a maximum of half to be restored. You are expected to behave and conform to prison rules throughout your sentence and that includes working regularly or attending educational classes. I am satisfied that the decision to restore 28 days was appropriate but generous in your case. In view of this your request for the restoration of further eligible days is refused.

SIGNATURE: P. Jones   DATE: 28/10/98
Governor.

REQUEST/COMPLAINT APPEAL FORM

THIS SECTION FOR OFFICIAL USE ONLY				
ESTABLISHMENT HMYOI CAMPING	CATEGORY YOI	STATUS CONV		DATE ISSUED 14/1/99
NAME BASHO		SERIAL NO 16/99		DATE RECEIVED 19/1/99
NUMBER VP4139	LOCATION C WING	DATE OF BIRTH 21-10-81	CROSS REF —	DATE REPLIED

GUIDANCE NOTES:
(Further information is given in the booklet "How to make a request or complaint")

1. You should use this form when you have already made a written request/complaint at your establishment, and you wish to appeal to HQ against the reply.

2. Please limit your appeal to one subject. It there are other matters which you wish to raise, ask for a separate request/complaint form.

3. Please write clearly. Do not use abusive or insulting language.

4. Please write in English if possible. (Welsh speaking inmates may write in Welsh). If you write in another language this could lead to delay.

GIVE YOUR REASONS FOR MAKING AN APPEAL   Serial No. of original request/complaint form: 752/98

I have been trying for several weeks to get on the Motor Mechanics Course. I've got a problem as I keep taking cars that don't belong to me, and my Probation Officer thinks I need help. This course will help me a lot. Anyway a vacancy came up and it was given to a white guy. Another place came up and although I was on the waiting list, it was given to another white guy. I don't think that is fair.

I saw the Race Relations Officer and he looked into the situation, but he

SIGNATURE: DATE:

(You may continue on the back if necessary)

F2059(B)

(APPEAL CONTINUED)

is racist too, and told me that the guys on the waiting list the longest were the ones who were offered the places. I don't think this is right, and I feel that I am being discriminated against because I am black. I want to appeal to the Area Manager in H.Q. because I can't get on this course and I'm only serving 12 months, so I won't be able to have a chance to sort myself out. Please help me.

SIGNATURE: *Judd Basho* DATE: 17/1/99

REPLY:

I have carefully looked into your complaint claiming that you suffered racial discrimination over your application to attend the Motor Mechanics Vocational Training Course which is very popular and oversubscribed. I consider that your application was processed properly but share the R.R.L.O.'s concern that non-white youngsters are under-represented. The Governor is addressing this issue as a matter of urgency. In view of your circumstances and the fact that your probation officer considers this course will help you address your offending behaviour, the Governor has decided that you should be given the next vacancy on the course.

SIGNATURE: *P. Cable* DATE: 15/2/1999

Area Manager (Central Region).

HM PRISON SERVICE

F1127 — NOTICE OF REPORT

Charge Number   286/97

Name .... NAUGHTIE ....   No .... KL 4653 ....

You have been placed on report by .... OFFICER SMITH ....
for the following alleged offence committed:

Time .... 1830hrs .... Date .... 15 SEPTEMBER 1997 ....

Place .... 'A' WING ....

Offence committed .... RULE 47 PARAGRAPH 1 ....
.... COMMITS ANY ASSAULT ....

Contrary to   Rule .... 47 .... Para .... 1 .... Prison/YOI Rules

Details of alleged offence

YOU DID ASSAULT KL 2764 PIGGOTT BY KICKING HIM AS HE LAY ON THE FLOOR AT THE FOOT OF THE STAIRS IN 'A' WING.

The Governor will hear your case at an adjudication at .... 1000 .. hrs on .... 16 SEPTEMBER 1997 ....
You will have every opportunity then to make your defence. If you wish to write out what you want to say you may do so on the back of this form. You or the governor may read it out at the hearing.
You may also state whether you wish to call any witnesses.

Issued at .... 0750 .... hrs   Date .... 16 SEPTEMBER 1997 ....

Name of issuing officer (block capitals) .... OFFICER JONES ....

Printed by PFS at HMP Leyhill ON001 (F1127 Rev 4/92) 6/95 XLY D182

HM PRISON SERVICE

Charge Number	286/97

F 254 - REPORT TO THE GOVERNOR OF ALLEGED OFFENCE BY INMATE

Inmate's Name ....NAUGHTIE................................ Number ....KL4653..............................

Details of alleged offence

Time ....1830............... hrs   Date ....15..SEPTEMBER..1997............................

Place ....'A' WING..

Offence committed ....` COMMIT ANY ASSAULT ....

....

....

Contrary to Rule....47.......... Para .....1........ Prison † / YOI † / Rules

Officer's Report

(Continue overleaf
if necessary)

At the time, date and place ststed, I saw KL 2764 NAUGHTIE
kicking inmate KL 2764 PIGGOTT as he lay on the floor at the
foot of the stairs. I shouted at KL 4653 NAUGHTIE to stop.
He turned to look at me, shouted abuse, and carried on kicking
KL 2764 PIGGOTT. I rang the alarm bell then intervened, and staff
arrived to help remove KL4653 NAUGHTIE to the segregation unit.
KL 2764 PIGGOTT was taken to the Health Care Centre for treatment.

Signature of officer ....Officer··Smith........................   Date .....15..September..97.........

Name (in capitals) ....OFFICER SMITH.................................   Rank ....OFFICER................

*To be completed if and when a Disciplinary Charge is Laid
†Delete if inapplicable

OT 002 (F254) (Rev 3/89) 4/95 HMP Maidstone

F256/OR001   Charge Number $\boxed{286/97}$

RECORD OF HEARING AND ADJUDICATION

Part 1 (to be completed in BLOCK CAPITALS before hearing)

1   Establishment: HM P *Camphill*

Date of Adjudication *16th September 1997*
(Commencement)

2   First name(s) *Paddy*   Surname *NAUGHTIE*

Number *KL4653* ~~Determinate Sentence~~ / Lifer / ~~Unsentenced~~ / ~~Non Criminal~~*
delete whichever is not applicable

3   Details of the charge (as recorded on F1127/ON001)

RULE 47 Para I · Commits Any Assault ,
You did assault KL 2764 Piggott by kicking him as he
lay at the ~~foot~~ of the stairs in 'A' Wing at 1630hrs on 15/9/97

F1127/ON001 - Issued by _____   Time and Date of Issue *0800*
Name of Reporting Officer *SMITH*   Rank *Officer*

4   Certification by Medical Officer : Please TICK appropriate box(es)

Fit for adjudication ☑   Fit for cellular confinement ☑   Unfit (give details below) ☐

Any relevant medical/psychiatric observations including an opinion on the prisoner's mental condition at the time of the alleged offence (a separate report should be attached if appropriate)

Signature of Medical Officer _____   Date *16/9/97*

5   Adjudicated by Governor ☑   Other Governor grade ☐ _____
(please specify)

Head of Custody ☐

If adjudication is not conducted by the governing governor or Head of Custody, please give reason:

A514

Part 2 PRELIMINARIES

6

Time commenced: 1030 hours

Please TICK this box to record a plea of not guilty if the inmate refuses to attend ☐

IDENTIFY THE PRISONER AND ASK THE FOLLOWING QUESTIONS
(please TICK prisoner's response)

	YES	NO
1 Have you received the Notice of Report form F1127/ON001?	✓	☐
2 Have you received F1145/OZ001 explaining how this hearing will proceed?	✓	☐
3 Do you understand the procedure?	✓	☐

CHARGE TO BE READ OUT AT THIS STAGE

	YES	NO
4 Do you understand the charge?	✓	☐
5 Have you made a written reply to the charge?	☐	✓
6 Have you had sufficient time to prepare your answer?	✓	☐
7 Do you want any additional help at this hearing? *(If yes, explain the possibilities of assistance by a friend or legal representative)*	☐	✓
8 Will you be calling any witnesses?	☐	✓

9 How do you plead: Guilty ✓ Not Guilty ☐ Not guilty owing to refusal to plead ☐

Part 3 RECORD OF HEARING

7

Record all salient points

Offr Smith : read out evidence (attached)

Gov: What injuries did KL 2764 Piggott receive?

Offr Smith: He received bruising to his back and legs. After treatment he was fit enough to return to the Wing.

Gov: Any questions for Offr Smith?

Naughtie: Did Offr Smith see how the fight started?

Off Smith: No; all I saw was you assaulting Piggott as stated in my evidence.

Gov: Anything you wish to say?

Naughtie: Yes Guv; it all started because he owed me money for tobacco and wouldn't pay me back. When he called me a 'nonce' I lost my temper and hit him.

Gov: You were provoked?

Naughtie: Yes Governor.

7 (cont)

> Governor: I am satisfied with the evidence I have heard and find the charge against you proved.

Continue on loose sheet F256A/OR005 if necessary and attach to inside of cover on completion.

Part 4 REFERRAL TO POLICE

8

Charge referred to police ☐	Date _____
Decision to prosecute ☐	Date _____
Decision not to prosecute ☐	Date _____

Part 5 OUTCOME

9 Date 16 | 9 | 97

Charge proved ☑   Charge dismissed ☐   Charge not proceeded with (give reason Part 3) ☐

10 If the finding was one of guilt, prisoner's plea in mitigation:
(If none, state none)

I'm sorry.

11 Report on conduct and previous record during current sentence to be read out at this stage.
Number of previous disciplinary reports (Findings of guilt only).......15.................
Does prisoner wish to add anything or ask any questions in connection with the report?   No.

Naughtie is serving a Life Sentence. 3 previous offences of a similar nature, the most recent 14/4/97 when he assaulted an officer. The wing state that he is moody but cooperative. He can be aggressive if he doesn't get his own way. Currently going through an argumentative phase.

Part 6 PUNISHMENT

12

| | If suspended state for how long (max 6 months) |

Caution ___—___ tick

Forfeiture of remission/Award of added days ___—___ days

Prospective forfeiture of remission/added days ___—___ days

Cellular confinement/confinement to room ___14___ days

Exclusion from associated work ___—___ days

Stoppage of earnings { period ___14___ days

percentage ___—___ %

Forfeiture of facilities (privileges)

Canteen/facilities to purchase/ use of private cash ___14___ days

Association/dining/recreation/entertaining/classes ___14___ days

Tobacco ___—___ days

Publications ___14___ days

Radio ___14___ days

Occupations in cell ___14___ days

Possessions in cell ___14___ days

Removal from activity (YOI) ___—___ days

Extra work (YOI) ___—___ days

Removal from wing/unit (YOI) ___—___ days

Other facilities (privileges) withdrawn ___ _____ ___

13 If the punishment above is **consecutive** to another,
insert other charge numbers: ___N/A___

If the punishment above is **concurrent** with another,
insert other charge numbers: ___N/A___

14 Are there any existing suspended punishments? Yes ☑ No ☐ *tick box*
If yes: Charge number __240/97__ Action taken __Not activated; not of__
__a similar nature__

15 PRISONER INFORMED OF PUNISHMENT AND ACTIVATION ☑ Date __16/9/97__

16 Signature of Governor _S.M. Gravett_
Name (use block capitals) __S.M.GRAVETT__ Date __16/9/97__

17 Finding and punishment, if any, entered in record F2050/BR010
Officer's Signature _A Brown_ Date __16/9/97__

LICENCE

Criminal Justice Act 1991

HM Prison / YOI ....

Name: Date of Birth:

Prison No: NIB No:

1.   Under the provisions of Section 33 (1)(b) of the Criminal Justice Act 1991 you are being released on licence. You will be under the supervision of a probation officer or a social worker of a local authority social services department and must comply with the conditions of this licence. The objectives of this supervision are to (a) protect the public, (b) prevent re-offending and (c) achieve your successful re-integration into the community.

2.   Your supervision commences on (date)
      and expires on (date)
      unless this licence is previously suspended.

3.   On release you must report without delay to

      (name)

      (address)

4.   You must place yourself under the supervision of whichever probation officer or social worker is nominated for this purpose from time to time.

5.   While under supervision you must:

      i.   keep in touch with your supervising officer in accordance with any reasonable instructions that you may from time to time be given;

      ii.   if required, receive visits from your supervising officer at your home at reasonable hours and for reasonable periods;

      iii.   live where reasonably approved by your supervising officer and notify him or her in advance of any proposed change of address;

      iv.   undertake only such employment as your supervising officer reasonably approves and notify him or her in advance of any proposed change in employment or occupation;

      v.   not travel outside the United Kingdom without obtaining the prior permission of your supervising officer;

vi.   not take any action which would jeopardise the objectives of your supervision, namely to protect the public, prevent you from re-offending and secure your successful reintegration into the community;

(vii.   Additional licence conditions)

6.   The Secretary of State may vary or cancel any of the above conditions, in accordance with Section 37 (5) of the Criminal Justice Act 1991.

7.   In accordance with the provisions of Section 38 of the Criminal Justice Act 1991, if you do not comply with the requirements in paragraphs 3,4 and 5 above you will be liable to prosecution before a court. The court may fine you up to level 3 on the standard scale and / or send you back to prison for the remaining period of your licence or for 6 months, if that is shorter. If you are sent back to prison and released before the end of your licence, you will still be subject to supervision.

8.   Your sentence expires on (date). In accordance with the provisions of Section 40 of the Criminal Justice Act 1991, you are liable to be returned to custody if you are convicted of a further imprisonable offence committed before your sentence has fully expired. The court dealing with the new offence may add all or part of the outstanding period of the original sentence onto any new sentence it may impose.

Signed: Status:

Date:

for the Secretary of State for the Home Department

This licence has been given to me and its requirements have been explained.

Signed:

Date:

HM PRISON SERVICE
SEX OFFENDERS WHO NEED TO REGISTER WITH THE POLICE
SEX OFFENDERS ACT 1997, PART 1, SCHEDULE 1

This notice summarises the notification requirements under the Sex Offenders Act as they apply to sex offenders who are in prison on 1 September 1997. It is not a complete statement of the law. If you need more help in understanding what is required you should obtain legal advice.

Offenders who come within the provisions of this Act must **by law** within 14 days of their date of release from prison:

- **notify the police** of their name, any other names they use, their date of birth and their home address (if they have no home address, they must give the address of any premises they regularly visit)

- **notify the police** of any change of name or home address within 14 days of the date of any change

- **notify the police** of any address where they reside or stay for 14 days or longer. This means either 14 days at a time, or a total of 14 days in any 12 month period.

Offenders can notify the police by either going or writing to a police station in the area in which their home is situated. The police will provide a written acknowledgement when this has been done.

Details of how long the requirement to notify lasts, and which offences the Act applies to, are set out overleaf.

It is a criminal offence, punishable with up to six months' imprisonment and/or a fine, to fail to comply with these requirements, or to give the police false information.

I have today given a copy of this notice to

Name of prisoner...

CRO number............................

Offence and date of offence...

....

Discharge address..

....

Signed..   Prison officer

Name..

Date............................

Establishment..

I have today received a copy of this notice

Signed ....   Date   ....

Copies to 1. Prisoner, 2. Prison Service records, 3. Police, 4. Probation.

SPECIMEN LIFE LICENCES

LICENCE

Criminal Justice Act 1991

The Secretary of State hereby authorises the release on licence within fifteen days of the date hereof of [NAME] who shall on release and during the period of this licence comply with the following conditions or any other condition which may be substituted or added from time to time.

1.   He shall place himself under the supervision of whichever probation officer is nominated for this purpose from time to time.

2.   He shall on release report to the probation officer so nominated, and shall keep in touch with that officer in accordance with that officer's instructions.

3.   He shall, if his probation officer so requires, receive visits from that officer where the licence holder is living.

4.   He shall reside only where approved by his probation officer.

5.   He shall work only where approved by his probation officer and shall inform his probation officer at once if he loses his job.

6.   He shall not travel outside Great Britain without the prior permission of his probation officer.

Unless revoked this licence remains in force indefinitely.

. . . . **on behalf of the Secretary of State**

PDP/

Home Office   Supervising Officer: . . . .
Abell House   . . . .
                            . . . .
                            . . . .

APPENDIX II

Addresses

This section contains useful addresses referred to in this book only and is not intended to be a detailed list. For further information the reader is advised to consult the relevant reference works.

Apex Trust, St Alphage House, Wingate Annex, 2 Fore Street, London EC2Y 5DA.

Assisted Prisoner Visits Unit, PO Box 2152, Birmingham B15 1SD.

Commission for Racial Equality, Elliot House, 10/12 Allington Street, London SW1E 5EH.

Criminal Injuries Compensation Board, Tay House, 300 Bath Street, Glasgow G2 4JR.

Home Office Library, 55 Queen's Anne Gate, London SW1H 9AT.

The Koestler Award Trust, 9 Birchmead Avenue, Pinner, Middlesex HA5 2BG.

NCVQ, 222 Euston Road, London NW1 2BZ.

New Bridge, 27a Medway Street, London SW1P 2BD.

Prisoner Location Service, PO Box 2152, Birmingham B15 1SD.

Prisons Ombudsman, Ashley House, 2 Monck Street, London SW1P 2BQ.

The Registrar of Civic Appeals, Royal Courts of Justice, Strand, London WC2A 2LL.

SCOTVEC, Hanover House, 24 Douglas Street, Glasgow G2 7NQ.

Secretary General, European Commission of Human Rights, Council of Europe, 67006 Strasbourg, France.

Index